MW00622788

American Birding Association
Field Guide to Birds of Oregon

American Birding Association

Field Guide

to Birds of

Oregon

Dave Irons

PHOTOGRAPHS BY
Brian E. Small
AND OTHERS

Scott & Nix, Inc.
NEW YORK

Contents

The American Birding Association inspires all people to enjoy and protect wild birds.

The ABA represents the North American birding community and supports birders through publications, conferences, workshops, events, partnerships, and networks.

The ABA's education programs promote birding skills, ornithological knowledge, and the development of and implementation of a conservation ethic.

The ABA encourages birders to apply their skills to help conserve birds and their habitats, and we represent the interests of birders in planning and legislative arenas.

We welcome all birders as members.

THE AMERICAN BIRDING ASSOCIATION
CODE OF ETHICS

Everyone who enjoys birds and birding must always respect wildlife, its environment, and the rights of others. In any conflict of interest between birds and birders, the welfare of the birds and their environment comes first.

CODE OF BIRDING ETHICS

1. Promote the welfare of birds and their environment.

1(a)Support the protection of important bird habitat.

1(b)To avoid stressing birds or exposing them to danger, exercise restraint and caution during observation, photography, sound recording, or filming.

Limit the use of recordings and other methods of attracting birds, and never use such methods in heavily birded areas, or for attracting any species that is Threatened, Endangered, or of Special Concern, or is rare in your local area; Keep well back from nests and nesting colonies, roosts, display areas, and important feeding sites. In such sensitive areas, if there is a need for extended observation, photography, filming, or recording, try to use a blind or hide, and take advantage of natural cover.

Use artificial light sparingly for filming or photography, especially for close-ups.

1(c) Before advertising the presence of a rare bird, evaluate the potential for disturbance to the bird, its surroundings, and other people in the area, and proceed only if access can be controlled, disturbance minimized, and permission has been obtained from private land-owners. The sites of rare nesting birds should be divulged only to the proper conservation authorities.

1(d) Stay on roads, trails, and paths where they exist; otherwise keep habitat disturbance to a minimum.

2. Respect the law, and the rights of others.

2(a) Do not enter private property without the owner's explicit permission.

2(b) Follow all laws, rules, and regulations governing use of roads and public areas, both at home and abroad.

2(c) Practice common courtesy in contacts with other people. Your exemplary behavior will generate goodwill with birders and non-birders alike.

3. Ensure that feeders, nest structures, and other artificial bird environments are safe.

3(a) Keep dispensers, water, and food clean, and free of decay or disease. It is important to feed birds continually during harsh weather.

3(b) Maintain and clean nest structures regularly.

3(c) If you are attracting birds to an area, ensure the birds are not exposed to predation from cats and other domestic animals, or dangers posed by artificial hazards.

4. Group birding, whether organized or impromptu, requires special care.

Each individual in the group, in addition to the obligations spelled out in Items 1 and 2, has responsibilities as a Group Member.

4(a)Respect the interests, rights, and skills of fellow birders, as well as people participating in other legitimate outdoor activities. Freely share your knowledge and experience, except where code 1(c) applies. Be especially helpful to beginning birders.

4(b)If you witness unethical birding behavior, assess the situation, and intervene if you think it prudent. When interceding, inform the person(s) of the inappropriate action, and attempt, within reason, to have it stopped. If the behavior continues, document it, and notify appropriate individuals or organizations.

Group Leader Responsibilities [amateur and professional trips and tours].

4(c)Be an exemplary ethical role model for the group. Teach through word and example.

4(d)Keep groups to a size that limits impact on the environment, and does not interfere with others using the same area.

4(e)Ensure everyone in the group knows of and practices this code.

4(f)Learn and inform the group of any special circumstances applicable to the areas being visited (e.g. no tape recorders allowed).

4(g)Acknowledge that professional tour companies bear a special responsibility to place the welfare of birds and the benefits of public knowledge ahead of the company's commercial interests. Ideally, leaders should keep track of tour sightings, document unusual occurrences, and submit records to appropriate organizations.

Everyone who enjoys birds and birding must always respect wildlife, its environment, and the rights of others. The ABA Code of Ethics should be read, followed, and shared by all birders.

Please follow this code and distribute and teach it to others.

The American Birding Association's Code of Birding Ethics may be freely reproduced for distribution/dissemination. An electronic version may be found at aba.org/about/ethics.

The American Birding Association inspires all people to enjoy and protect wild birds.

The ABA represents the North American birding community and supports birders through publications, conferences, workshops, events, partnerships, and networks.

The ABA's education programs promote birding skills, ornithological knowledge, and the development of and implementation of a conservation ethic.

The ABA encourages birders to apply their skills to help conserve birds and their habitats, and we represent the interests of birders in planning and legislative arenas.

We welcome all birders as members.

THE AMERICAN BIRDING ASSOCIATION
CODE OF ETHICS

Everyone who enjoys birds and birding must always respect wildlife, its environment, and the rights of others. In any conflict of interest between birds and birders, the welfare of the birds and their environment comes first.

CODE OF BIRDING ETHICS

1. Promote the welfare of birds and their environment.

1(a) Support the protection of important bird habitat.

1(b) To avoid stressing birds or exposing them to danger, exercise restraint and caution during observation, photography, sound recording, or filming.

Limit the use of recordings and other methods of attracting birds, and never use such methods in heavily birded areas, or for attracting any species that is Threatened, Endangered, or of Special Concern, or is rare in your local area; Keep well back from nests and nesting colonies, roosts, display areas, and important feeding sites. In such sensitive areas, if there is a need for extended observation, photography, filming, or recording, try to use a blind or hide, and take advantage of natural cover.

Use artificial light sparingly for filming or photography, especially for close-ups.

1(c) Before advertising the presence of a rare bird, evaluate the potential for disturbance to the bird, its surroundings, and other people in the area, and proceed only if access can be controlled, disturbance minimized, and permission has been obtained from private land-owners. The sites of rare nesting birds should be divulged only to the proper conservation authorities.

1(d) Stay on roads, trails, and paths where they exist; otherwise keep habitat disturbance to a minimum.

2. Respect the law, and the rights of others.

2(a) Do not enter private property without the owner's explicit permission.

2(b) Follow all laws, rules, and regulations governing use of roads and public areas, both at home and abroad.

2(c) Practice common courtesy in contacts with other people. Your exemplary behavior will generate goodwill with birders and non-birders alike.

3. Ensure that feeders, nest structures, and other artificial bird environments are safe.

3(a) Keep dispensers, water, and food clean, and free of decay or disease. It is important to feed birds continually during harsh weather.

3(b) Maintain and clean nest structures regularly.

3(c) If you are attracting birds to an area, ensure the birds are not exposed to predation from cats and other domestic animals, or dangers posed by artificial hazards.

4. Group birding, whether organized or impromptu, requires special care.

Each individual in the group, in addition to the obligations spelled out in Items 1 and 2, has responsibilities as a Group Member.

4(a)Respect the interests, rights, and skills of fellow birders, as well as people participating in other legitimate outdoor activities. Freely share your knowledge and experience, except where code 1(c) applies. Be especially helpful to beginning birders.

4(b)If you witness unethical birding behavior, assess the situation, and intervene if you think it prudent. When interceding, inform the person(s) of the inappropriate action, and attempt, within reason, to have it stopped. If the behavior continues, document it, and notify appropriate individuals or organizations.

Group Leader Responsibilities [amateur and professional trips and tours].

4(c)Be an exemplary ethical role model for the group. Teach through word and example.

4(d)Keep groups to a size that limits impact on the environment, and does not interfere with others using the same area.

4(e)Ensure everyone in the group knows of and practices this code.

4(f)Learn and inform the group of any special circumstances applicable to the areas being visited (e.g. no tape recorders allowed).

4(g)Acknowledge that professional tour companies bear a special responsibility to place the welfare of birds and the benefits of public knowledge ahead of the company's commercial interests. Ideally, leaders should keep track of tour sightings, document unusual occurrences, and submit records to appropriate organizations.

Everyone who enjoys birds and birding must always respect wildlife, its environment, and the rights of others. The ABA Code of Ethics should be read, followed, and shared by all birders.

Please follow this code and distribute and teach it to others.

The American Birding Association's Code of Birding Ethics may be freely reproduced for distribution/dissemination. An electronic version may be found at aba.org/about/ethics.

Foreword

Oregon is truly a great state for birding. From the Pacific bays, inlets, and beaches, the temperate rainforests of the coastal range to the Willamette Valley, the Columbia Plateau, the eastern Cascades and everywhere inbetween. Oregon really has a wealth of prime habitats for birds and outstanding oppurtunities for birders of all levels.

Like all the guides in this series, this book can help you do whatever you want with birding. Perhaps you enjoy birds a few days a year in your yard or local park and just want to know a little more about them and to know some of their names. Or maybe you want to dive deeper and really get familiar with the hundreds of amazing birds that call Oregon home for part or all of each year. Our aim is to meet you where you are and give you useful, reliable information and insight into birds and birding.

Author Dave Irons is the perfect guide for those wanting to explore the birds of Oregon. You're in very good hands with him. The gorgeous photography by Brian E. Small and others will not only to aid your identifications—it will inspire you to get out and see more of these beautiful and fascinating creatures for yourself.

I invite you to visit the American Birding Association website (aba.org), where you'll find a wealth of free resources and ways to connect with the birding community that will also help you get the most from your birding in Oregon and beyond. Please consider becoming an ABA member yourself—one of the best parts of birding is joining a community of fun, passionate people.

Now get on out there! Enjoy this book. Enjoy Oregon. And most of all, enjoy birding!

Good birding,

Jeffrey A. Gordon

Jeffrey A. Gordon, *President*
American Birding Association

A Pacific Wonderland for Birds

For many decades the bottom of Oregon license plates read "Pacific Wonderland." Oregon is surely that and so much more. Stretching nearly 400 miles east to west and 300 miles north to south, Oregon is the ninth largest state in land area. Nearly ninety percent of the human population lives in the western third, west of the Cascades Range. Western Oregon is very much the place one sees on postcards and travel brochures: lush, green, and heavily forested, with waterfalls, snow-capped volcanic peaks, and rugged coastlines. Fast-moving mountain streams wind down out of the mountains, feeding rivers that flow into the mighty Columbia, which ultimately empties into the Pacific Ocean.

In winter, western Oregon sees frequent, sometimes incessant rain, but it is mostly soft and steady, with skin-soaking downpours the exception. Temperatures at lower elevations

The Western Meadowlark–Oregon's state bird–has a remarkably powerful voice. Its rich bubbling song can be easily heard from a quarter mile away.

rarely drop below freezing. Summer weather here is as close to perfect as it is anywhere: there is little if any rainfall, and high temperatures are generally comfortable. Humidity is low, and Pacific breezes keep the air moving.

The eastern two-thirds of Oregon is largely rural. Three counties here have human populations of less than than 2000; Harney County, Oregon's largest by area, has only about 7500 inhabitants.

Lying in the rain shadow of the Cascades, central and eastern Oregon are arid and sometimes unforgiving landscapes. The moderating effects of the Pacific Ocean are mostly unfelt here, and temperature extremes mirror those in the mid-section of the continent, particularly in winter. Much of the land is treeless or nearly so. Crops require intense irrigation. Runoff from the mountains of southeastern Oregon flows into closed playa lakes, where it evaporates quickly in the low relative humidity.

You may not need rain gear while birding in eastern and central Oregon, but close attention to logistics will be critical. Conveniences such as gas, food, lodging, emergency medical care, and even a hot cup of coffee are not available on every corner. Cell phone service is far from a given, making good maps or GPS a necessity. But there are plenty of publicly owned Forest Service and Bureau of Land Management lands to explore. Campgrounds are plentiful, generally rustic, and relatively uncrowded.

The Scope of this Guide

About 540 species of birds have been recorded in Oregon, but many are rare or hard to find. This book features nearly 300 species and subspecies that occur regularly in the state, including year-round residents, breeding birds found only in spring and summer, and birds that only winter in Oregon. You will also find a handful of species that migrate through the state at predictable times in spring or fall each year.

Getting Started

Appreciating birds requires little more than your eyes and ears. You can look at a Lazuli Bunting and marvel at its beauty without knowing what it is called. You can hear the fluting song of a Swainson's Thrush and have it bring you joy even if you don't know the name of the singer. But there is something in humans that makes us eventually ask, "What is that bird?"

Once you start not just looking at birds but trying to identify them, you will probably want a pair of binoculars. Starting out in the $250–400 range will get you a pair that enhances your enjoyment and will last through the early years of your newfound hobby. Magnifications of 7x or 8x are ideal. Remember that higher magnification translates to more weight: birding won't be as much fun if your neck hurts.

This field guide is meant as an accessible and digestible reference to Oregon's most common birds. As you become familiar with the birds in this book or start to travel outside of the state for birding, you may want to "graduate" to a more comprehensive field guide covering more species.

Identifying Birds

When you are starting out, most birds will be identified by sight. Don't get lost in the details of color, pattern, and "field marks." Instead, begin to identify an unknown bird by looking at its relative size, shape, and bill type.

SIZE

Most of us can recognize a few kinds of birds already. Use that knowledge to help gauge the size of an unknown bird: Is it smaller than, larger than, or about the same size as a robin, a crow, or a hawk? As you learn to recognize more birds, add them to your mental catalogue of size references. Rapid assessment of size will become something you do without even thinking about it.

SHAPE

There are nearly as many bird shapes as there are birds. Again, make comparisons with birds that you already know. Though they are close in size, for example, the shape of an American Robin is quite different from the shape of a California Scrub-Jay. Some birds, like robins, are plump, while others, like scrub jays, are slender. Some have long necks, some appear almost neckless. Some birds are pot-bellied. Some have stubby legs or small feet, while others have gangly legs and long toes.

You can also compare a bird to itself. For instance, you might notice that the tail is as long as the body, or that the bill is half the front-to-rear length of the head. A bird can look proportionally large-headed and short-tailed, like a Hammond's Flycatcher, or smaller-headed and longer-tailed, like a Dusky Flycatcher. Over time, comparisons like this will become automatic. You will gradually develop search images tied to the shape and structural features of a bird, often allowing you to identify it without seeing any color or pattern at all.

From May–July no bird will be heard more frequently in the Coast Range than the Swainson's Thrush. Using a double voice box to sing two sets of notes simultaneously, this secretive forest bird creates a unique ethereal upward spiraling song.

BILL

The shape of a bird's bill can tell us what it eats and how it gets its food. Cone-shaped bills, such as those of sparrows, finches, grosbeaks, and buntings, are typically used for crushing or breaking open seeds. The short, thin bills of such birds as warblers, flycatchers, and some small sandpipers are suited to picking up insects and other soft foods. Birds with longer, thinner bills are more likely to be seen probing bark or the ground, as do many shorebirds, woodpeckers, thrashers, and nuthatches. Hawks, owls, and eagles have strong, hooked bills. It is often easiest to assess the length of a bird's bill by comparing it to other parts of the bird's body.

Identifying Birds by Sound

Different people learn bird songs and calls in different ways. Some can memorize bird sounds by listening to recordings, but for most us, the best way to learn is to track the bird down and watch it sing or call.

SONG

A bird's song is typically a series of notes or multi-note phrases repeated in a fixed sequence. Most birds sing only on the breeding grounds, where song is used to attract mates and to mark and defend territories.

Many birds include snippets of other species' vocalizations in their songs. Catbirds, mockingbirds, and thrashers are excellent imitators, as is the European Starling. Oregon's notable mimics also include the Cassin's Finch and Lesser Goldfinch.

CALLS

Calls are generally shorter and less complex than songs, most of them made up of only one or two notes. Calls can serve a variety of functions. Alarm calls, such as the high-pitched fast trills of chickadees and bushtits, alert other birds to the presence of a predator. Scolding calls, usually raspy and loud, may be used to distract or intimidate a predator. Other calls, such as the chatter of feeding shorebirds or the flight calls of migrating songbirds, help maintain contact among individuals.

Parts of a Bird

The following illustrations with captions point out the prominent aspects of four major groups of birds.

PARTS A SONGBIRD
This adult White-crowned Sparrow shows major body parts and field marks of a perched songbird.

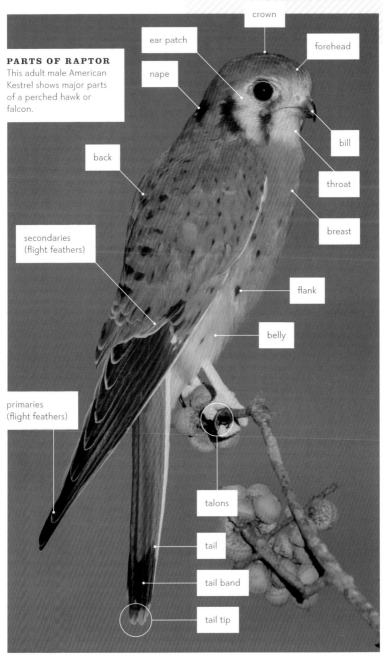

crown

ear patch

forehead

PARTS OF RAPTOR
This adult male American
Kestrel shows major parts
of a perched hawk or
falcon.

nape

bill

throat

back

breast

secondaries
(flight feathers)

flank

belly

primaries
(flight feathers)

talons

tail

tail band

tail tip

PARTS OF A DUCK
This adult male Northern Pintail shows major parts of a duck's body as it rests on the water.

PARTS OF A GULL
This adult Western Gull in summer plumage shows colors and some body parts visible on a gull or shorebird as it rests on a beach.

Oregon's Birding Regions

THE COAST

Millions of waterfowl, seabirds, and shorebirds occur along Oregon's Pacific coast, where rocky headlands and sea stacks are home to massive colonies of breeding alcids, cormorants, and gulls. Spring migration on the coast peaks during a brief period from late April to mid-May, but fall migration is much more extended. Southbound adult shorebirds are on the move by early July, followed by their offspring a month later. The southbound movements of waterfowl, loons, and gulls stretch into early November. In the non-nesting season, from September to April, sheltered bays and expansive estuaries are heavily used by ducks, gulls, and other water birds.

THE COAST RANGE

The low-lying Coast Range divides the outer coast from the valleys west of the Cascades. As the first ridgeline to wring water out of clouds rolling in from the ocean, it is covered by a dense, moist forest of Douglas-fir, western red cedar, red alder, and bigleaf maple. Noble fir, otherwise rare in Oregon, covers the summit of Marys Peak, at 4,098 feet the highest point in the Coast Range. The best time to bird the Coast Range is from May to July; this is a great place to find Mountain Quail and Sooty Grouse.

THE SISKIYOU MOUNTAINS

The northwest extension of the Klamath Mountains, the Siskiyous are rugged mountains with several peaks over 7,000 feet. Much of this area is federally designated wilderness, accessible only to hikers. Spring and summer are the best time to visit, but the road to the Mt. Ashland Ski Area is maintained in the winter.

THE WILLAMETTE VALLEY

Skinner Butte in downtown Eugene and Mt. Tabor Park on Portland's densely populated east side are popular spots to observe the spring migration. Portland's 5,200-acre Forest Park is one of the largest "urban forests" in the country. The Willamette Valley also has a network of National Wildlife Refuges (Ankeny, Baskett Slough, and William L. Finley) set aside for wintering "Dusky" Canada Geese; the fields and wetlands here attract hundreds of thousands of wintering waterfowl, along with raptors and song birds. State wildlife areas at

Fern Ridge Reservoir near Eugene and on Sauvie Island north of
Portland attract nesting ducks and marsh birds in spring and summer
and migrant shorebirds from July to September.

THE SOUTHWESTERN VALLEYS

The Umpqua and Rogue Valleys, separated from the Willamette Valley
by the Calapooya Mountains, are considerably drier, with more pine,
oak, madrone, and brushy understory. Nashville Warblers nest
commonly in the foothills. The Rogue Valley is especially arid. The
foothills around Medford and Ashland are clad in chaparral-type
habitat with breeding Ash-throated Flycatcher, Juniper Titmouse,
Blue-gray Gnatcatcher, California Towhee, and Lark Sparrow, all
species not regularly found elsewhere in western Oregon.

THE CASCADES

Stretching from the Columbia River to the California border and up
to ninety miles wide in places, the Cascades are the state's tallest
mountains, covering about 17 percent of Oregon's total area. Rainfall
and snowfall are much greater on the western slope, resulting in
dense vegetation dominated by firs, cedars, alders, vine maple,
rhododendrons, and ferns. Common to abundant birds in these
forests include the Pacific-slope Flycatcher, Steller's Jay, Chestnut-
backed Chickadee, Swainson's Thrush, Pacific Wren, and Hermit and
Wilson's Warblers.

When birders come
to visit Oregon, the
Hermit Warbler is
always near the top
of the list of the birds
they want to see.

The drier, eastern slopes of the Cascades are covered with more open forests of lodgepole and ponderosa pines and western juniper. The brushy understory is shorter and more patchy, featuring manzanita, ceanothus, and bitterbrush. Dusky and Gray Flycatchers, White-headed Woodpecker, Williamson's Sapsucker, Mountain Chickadee, Pgymy Nuthatch, and Cassin's Finch are characteristic of these pine forests, but are not found in the wetter fir forests just a few miles to the west.

THE COLUMBIA PLATEAU

The Oregon portion of the Columbia Plateau lies between the Cascades and the Blue Mountains and north of the Ochoco Mountains east of Prineville. Much of the Plateau is given over to wheat monoculture, with occasional patches of shrub-steppe and riparian corridors along the Deschutes, John Day, and Umatilla Rivers. The many small pothole marshes support a few pairs of breeding Cinnamon Teal and Gadwall, coots and rails, and modest numbers of Yellow-headed Blackbirds; a few of these marshes have Tricolored Blackbirds. Some of the birds that thrive in drier upland areas are the Swainson's Hawk, Long-billed Curlew, Horned Lark, and Vesper Sparrow.

Few waterfowl rival the beauty of a male Cinnamon Teal. This species breeds commonly in the pothole marshes of the Columbia Plateau.

THE HIGH DESERT

This region, the northern edge of the Great Basin in eastern Klamath, Lake, Harney, Malheur, and southern Deschutes Counties, sees annual precipitation of about 15 inches, making it far more arid than any other part of Oregon. The vegetation here is predominantly sagebrush steppe, with extensive stands of western juniper in the transition zones where the Cascades, Ochocos, and Blue Mountains meet the high plateau. The most numerous birds here, at an average elevation of 4,000 feet, are the Sage Thrasher, Gray Flycatcher, and the ubiquitous Brewer's Sparrow.

BASIN AND RANGE

This is a series of north-south mountains and modest mountain ranges within the high desert of southeastern Oregon. The playa-like basins in between fill with water in spring and early summer, creating extensive marshes with large breeding populations of waterfowl, herons and ibis, shorebirds, and uncountable numbers of Red-winged and Yellow-headed Blackbirds.

Brewer's Sparrow is among the most abundant breeding birds in Oregon's sagebrush steppe country. It makes up for it drab appearance with a long complex buzzy song that rings out over the sage.

Rising to nearly 10,000 feet, Steens Mountain is the most impressive geologic feature in the region. The snowmelt from Steens feeds Malheur National Wildlife Refuge and one of the largest freshwater marsh systems in the world. In contrast, the Alvord Basin, which lies in the rain shadow of Steens Mountain, gets a mere seven inches of annual rainfall and receives virtually none of the mountain's spring and summer runoff. The white, mostly dry alkali lake bed of Alvord Lake is starkly different from the lush Blitzen Valley on the other side of the mountain.

KLAMATH BASIN

The Klamath Basin is fed by snowmelt from the Cascades, which helps maintain Upper Klamath Lake and the year-round flow of the Klamath River. Unlike the more easterly basins, Klamath remains full of water through the winter, when it supports many waterfowl and raptors. From late February through April, few places in North America can rival the Klamath Basin's spectacle of hundreds of thousands of Snow, Ross's, and Greater White-fronted Geese on their way to the arctic breeding grounds; duck numbers are even more impressive. Bald Eagles congregate here by the hundreds, assembling each night at Bear Valley to form the largest eagle roost in the Lower 48.

THE NORTHEAST MOUNTAINS

The Blue and Wallowa Mountains of northeastern Oregon are geographically connected to the Rocky Mountains and share much of their wildlife. Among the species not found in the Cascades or elsewhere in eastern Oregon are the Spruce Grouse, Dusky Grouse, and Pine Grosbeak. In winter, this corner of the state regularly sees boreal species such as the White-winged Crossbill and Common Redpoll, along with a large influx of Bohemian Waxwings.

The Oregon Birding Year

JANUARY–FEBRUARY With planning and effort it is possible to amass a list of 100 or more species in a day in western Oregon even in the dead of winter. The Willamette Valley's state and federal refuges are teeming with waterfowl and raptors. Coastal pastures and estuaries offer great opportunities to hone your skills in gull identification. This is also the time to visit Union and Wallowa Counties for the best chances at such boreal and montane species as Bohemian Waxwing, Common Redpoll, Gray-crowned Rosy-Finch, Pine Grosbeak, and White-winged Crossbill; a Gyrfalcon often winters in the open country north and east of Joseph in Wallowa County. The first Rufous Hummingbirds typically reach the southern Oregon coast in late February.

MARCH Waterfowl are on the move north. Massive numbers of Snow, Ross's, and Greater White-fronted Geese gather in the Klamath, Summer Lake, and Harney Basins, to fatten up for the long flight to Alaska and northern Canada. The Bald Eagle roost at Bear Valley remains active well into March. Rufous Hummingbirds arrive at feeders along the coast and throughout the western lowlands. Orange-crowned Warblers are conspicuous by the end of March, particularly on the outer coast. East of the Cascades, the first northbound songbirds include Say's Phoebes, Mountain Bluebirds, and Townsend's Solitaires.

Once critically endangered and on a path to extinction, the Bald Eagle has rallied back and is once again a fixture in the skies over Oregon.

APRIL   Western Oregon birders anxiously await the first Hammond's Flycatcher or Black-throated Gray Warbler. In Portland, Mt. Tabor Park and Pittock Mansion are the best places to sample migration. Skinner's Butte at the edge of downtown Eugene is the premier spring migrant site in the southern Willamette Valley. Many flycatchers, vireos, and warblers arrive by the third week of April. During peak flights, usually in the last four or five days of April, tens of thousands of Western Sandpipers, Dunlins, Short-billed Dowitchers, and Black-bellied and Semipalmated Plovers can be seen at close range at low tide on the beach between Gearhart and the mouth of the Columbia River.

MAY   West of the Cascades, shorebird and songbird migration remains strong through the first two weeks of May. Large numbers of Whimbrels and Sanderlings move through in early May with a few Marbled Godwits, Ruddy Turnstones, and Red Knots. On the east side, mid-May is the perfect time to visit pine forests on the east slope of the Cascades or venture into the sagebrush steppe of the high desert. For many Oregon birders, Memorial Day weekend means a trip to Malheur National Wildlife Refuge for breeding marsh birds and flocks of migrants.

JUNE   June and July are perhaps the best birding months in Oregon. During the first week or two of June, Malheur is a prime site for late songbird migrants. Pine and fir forests on the eastern slope of the Cascades boast an unrivaled roster of breeding woodpeckers.

The nine-foot wingspan of a the American White Pelican is the longest of any Oregon bird. They have multiple breeding colonies along the Columbia River and in the Great Basin.

JULY The North American record for a July "big day"—the attempt to see and hear as many species as possible in a single twenty-four-hour period—was set in Oregon, proof of how good July birding is in the state. Along the outer coast, the first southbound shorebirds show up by the first week of the month. The edges of interior reservoirs and lakes can also be productive, with Summer Lake Wildlife Management Area among the best of many excellent shorebird sites. By mid-July, nearly all the higher-elevation roads are free of snow. The begging calls of the young make it easier to find American Three-toed and Black-backed Woodpeckers and other normally secretive species.

AUGUST Nesting activity wanes by early August, but a trip to higher, cooler elevations can still offer productive birding. Along the coast, juvenile shorebirds flood south from the Arctic, while thousands of California Gulls pour out of their interior breeding areas to mass on beaches with hordes of Brown Pelicans and Heerman's Gulls dispersing from the south. The road to the summit of Steens Mountain is usually open by early August, providing access to Oregon's only Black Rosy-Finches.

SEPTEMBER Shorebirds and waterfowl are conspicuous, particularly around coastal estuaries. Nearshore movements of loons, scoters, shearwaters, gulls, and terns make seawatching a must, and this is the best month of the year for an offshore boat trip in search of Sabine's Gulls, shearwaters, albatrosses, jaegers, and alcids. Overwintering Golden-crowned and Fox Sparrows

The Black-backed Woodpecker is generally scarce and hard to find in living forests, but after montane wildfires they can be the most abundant woodpecker in charred stands of pine and fir.

arrive in good numbers by the end of the month, while the first southbound Cackling Geese are back at the Willamette Valley refuges by mid-September. The last ten days of September often sees a massive flight of Greater White-fronted Geese over the Willamette Valley. September is also a great time for Malheur National Wildlife Refuge and other eastside oases. Migrant songbirds, particularly Yellow-rumped Warblers and White-crowned Sparrows, can be too numerous to count on some days, along with a nice mix of other warblers, sparrows, tanagers, vireos, and flycatchers.

OCTOBER   The onset of the wet season refills many swales and seasonal puddles, and geese and ducks will be abundant in good habitat. Scoters and gulls continue to move along the outer coast, with sometimes astounding flights of southbound Pacific Loons. Strong storms can push some seabirds inshore that are otherwise rarely seen from land.

NOVEMBER   Wintering sparrows abound in rural hedgerows and blackberry thickets. Coastal estuaries are filled with Common Loons, Horned Grebes, scoters, mergansers, and other ducks. Hawks and eagles are common in the westside lowlands and the open country east of the Cascades. Columbia River dams can host large rafts of diving ducks, mostly Lesser and Greater Scaup, and wintering gulls.

DECEMBER   By December, migration is essentially over for songbirds. Trees or berry patches that still have fruit and back-yard bird feeding stations are sure to attract a crowd. Weedy garden plots and truck farms with leftover rotting produce are also worth exploring, as they typically attract large mixed flocks of sparrows, juncos, and finches. It is also the time when lingering "semi-hardy" warblers like Townsend's and Yellow-rumped come to suet feeders, replacing protein in their diet that would usually come from insects. Don't underestimate the potential of birding close to home. Midwinter walks through residential neighbor-hoods can be quite productive. Look for mixed feeding flocks of chickadees, nuthatches and kinglets, as they may be joined by the occasional vagrant or out of season warbler. Hummingbird feeders will be appreciated by Anna's Hummingbirds, which don't leave for the winter. Hummer feeders occasionally attract overwintering orioles.

How to Use This Guide

SPECIES ACCOUNTS

Each species account is headed with the bird's common and scientific names. The scientific names may seem unfamiliar, but they contain important information about how species are related to each other. These names are made up of two words, the second, uncapitalized word identifying the species and the first, capitalized word naming the genus, which is a group of closely related species. For example, the American Redstart *Setophaga ruticilla* and the Hermit Warbler *Setophaga occidentalis* are in the same genus, *Setophaga*, a close relationship concealed by their English names.

The length and wingspan measurements are averages. The length figure indicates the distance from bill tip to tail tip, wingspan the distance from wingtip to wingtip on a fully extended wing. Absolute measurements cannot be assessed in the field. Furthermore, remember that size can vary individually or by sex. The figures given here are meant as a basis for comparison.

Each account includes a description of the bird's habitat and geographic distribution in Oregon. For some less common or less widespread species, particular sites are mentioned where the bird is likely to be seen. Unique feeding strategies, flight styles, and other behaviors that can help in identification are also described.

Most of the accounts end with a short description of the bird's vocalizations, both songs and call notes.

PHOTOS AND CAPTIONS

When adult males and females, or adults and immatures, differ noticeably in plumage, photos of both sexes or ages are included. Some species require more photos to accurately depict regional or individual variation.

Additional Resources

A variety of print and digital resources can help you learn, but there is no substitute for time in the field looking at birds in the company of knowledgeable, experienced birders. Find a mentor, or several mentors, and go birding with them as often as you can.

Eventually you may want a guide that covers all of the birds of North America. *The National Geographic Field Guide to the Birds of North America*, by Jon Dunn and Jonathan Alderfer, and the *Sibley Guide to Birds*, by David Sibley, are the standards. Though it is now over fifteen years old, *Birds of Oregon: A General Reference*, edited by Marshall, Hunter, and Contreras, is a still unmatched handbook of the life history, status, distribution, and seasonality of Oregon's birds.

Oregon Birders Online (orbirds.org/obolguidelines) is the oldest and largest listserv for Oregon birders. It's a great site for keeping up with the latest bird sightings in Oregon. If you do find a mentor, ask them which other websites they find useful.

If you are interested in field trips or birding classes, your local Audubon chapter is a great place to start. The Audubon Society of Portland offers an extensive slate of courses that combine a classroom experience with a field trip.

The Oregon Birding Association (orbirds.org), a statewide organization, holds a meeting in a different location each year, with numerous field trips timed to take advantage of the best local birding experiences. The organization's journal, *Oregon Birds*, publishes identification articles and site guides, along with field notes for the entire state.

EBird.org is a global database for bird records, co-sponsored by the Cornell Lab of Ornithology and the National Audubon Society. Anyone can join to submit and archive their own sightings. Your local eBird reviewer is likely to become yet another important mentor as you learn more about the birds of your area and state.

Glossary

BAND Broad horizontal stripe extending across a part of the bird, usually the tail or breast.

BAR Narrow horizontal stripe or line.

BREEDER Species known to nest.

BREEDING PLUMAGE Usually more colorful than non-breeding plumage.

BUFF Warm tan or tawny brown.

CALL Simple, one- or two-note vocalization serving a purpose other than territorial declaration or courtship. Some species have several different call notes.

CANOPY The umbrella-like structure of branches and foliage in the top of large deciduous trees. Where several trees overlap and touch, their upper branches form a "closed canopy."

CHESTNUT Dark reddish brown.

CINNAMON Warm orangish brown.

COMMON Always present, year-round or at the appropriate season. Expect more than one individual on every visit.

COVERTS Group of feathers protecting the area where longer, more rigid feathers connect to the skeleton. Primary coverts, for example, protect the base of a bird's outer wing feathers where they connect to wing bones.

DRUMMING Loud, rapid tapping by woodpeckers, analogous to other bird's songs.

EYE ARCS Contrasting semi-circles, usually paler than the rest of the face, above and below the eye that do not form a complete ring. A broken eye ring.

EYE RING Contrasting circle, usually paler than the rest of the face, completely around the eye.

FLIGHT CALL Typically single-note vocalization heard from flying birds.

FLIGHT FEATHERS Long, broad, stiff feathers making up most of the surface of a bird's wing. Primaries are the outermost nine or ten flight feathers; secondaries are the flight feathers of the inner portion of the wing.

GLIDE   Brief mid-flight pause with no wingbeats, typically on a horizontal or slightly downward trajectory.

GORGET   Patch of iridescent feathers on the throat of a humming-bird.

HAWKWATCH   Site where trained observers count and identify migrant raptors. Hawkwatch Interational runs fall monitoring stations all across the Americas, including one on Oregon's Bonney Butte.

HYBRID   Offspring resulting from the interbreeding of parents of two different species.

IMMATURE   Bird whose appearance is not yet adult-like. All juveniles are immatures, but not all immatures are juveniles.

IRIDESCENCE   Colors created by refraction from the surface of a feather, changing with the angle of view.

The brightly iridescent patch of throat feathers on this male Anna's Hummingbird is referred to as a gorget.

JUVENILE Bird still wearing its first full set of feathers, or the plumage of that bird.

MANTLE Feathers of the back and upperwing coverts taken together.

MOLT Regular shedding and replacement of feathers. Almost all birds grow a new set of feathers each year, usually in late summer or early fall.

MORPH Color variant within a species.

NAIL Dark tip on the bill of a duck.

N.W.R. National Wildlife Refuge.

PLUMAGE Complete set of feathers.

PRIMARY PROJECTION Distance between tip of the longest primary and tip of the longest secondary when the wing is folded.

RAPTOR Diurnal bird of prey, including hawks, eagles, Osprey, and falcons.

RARE Unlikely to be seen more than once or twice a year, and not always present at a given location.

RESIDENT Species that spends entire life in a relatively small area without regular seasonal movements.

SHAFT Rigid "stem" that anchors a feather in the body and supports webbing on both sides.

SONG Complex, multi-note vocalization mostly heard on breeding grounds.

STREAK Narrow line contrasting with the base color, formed by a row of vertically aligned dark marks on feathers.

SUBSPECIES Distinct population within a species.

UNCOMMON Present or likely present year-round or at the appropriate season, but not reliably seen on every visit.

UNDERPARTS Throat, breast, belly, and undertail, taken together.

UPPER PARTS   Back, wings, and rump, taken together.

UNDERWING   Underside of the wing.

WING BAR   White or pale bar across the folded wing, formed by pale tips on wing coverts.

WING LINING   Underwing coverts.

WING STRIPE   Diffuse pale or white stripe across flight feathers or wing coverts, usually visible only in flight.

W.M.A.   State-owned Wildlife Management Area.

American Birding Association

Field Guide to
Birds of Oregon

Greater White-fronted Goose

Anser albifrons

L 25-32 | **WS** 53"

Only modest numbers of Greater White-fronted Geese winter in Oregon, but migrating flocks can be spectacular at favored sites, with tens of thousands staging in the Klamath and Harney Basins in March and April before the long journey to their Arctic breeding grounds. Smaller numbers stop over at the Willamette Valley refuges and coastal pastures during both northbound and southbound migrations. They are high fliers when migrating, forming broad overlapping arcs rather than the "V" formation of Canada and Cackling Geese. Their loud two-note calls, which have a laughing quality, can be heard even when the birds themselves can barely be seen.

Adult. Mostly gray-brown, with orange legs and feet. Variable black splotching on paler breast. Bill pinkish orange with white feathering around the base.

Immature. Like adult, but lacks black splotching below. Little or no white around the base of the bill.

Snow Goose

Chen caerulescens

L 30" | **WS** 54"

The cacophony accompanying the liftoff of tens of thousands of white geese over Klamath Basin is a must-see and must-hear birding spectacle. From February to mid-April the Klamath, Harney, Summer Lake, and Warner Basins are staging sites for northbound Snow and Ross's Geese. In recent years the Pacific Flyway population has greatly increased, and Snow Geese are now frequently encountered in the Willamette Valley, particularly at Sauvie Island, where wintering flocks number in the thousands. The tight flocks can look like a blanket of snow from a distance. Some Snow Geese of the "blue" morph are seen in migration in the Klamath and Harney basins; this dark-bodied, white-headed variant is rare west of the Cascades.

Adult. Unlike the domestic forms of white geese in parks and barnyards, Snow Geese have distinctive black wingtips.

Adult "Blue Goose." This color variant has a dark slate-gray body and wings, but the white head and neck of a typical white Snow Goose.

Brant
Branta bernicla

L 22-26" | **WS** 45"

This mid-sized dark goose is found almost exclusively along the outer coast, where it occurs mostly as a migrant. Brant feed in estuarine shallows and on tidal mudflats, especially those covered in eel grass. Unlike other geese, Brant fly low over the open ocean in long straight lines. Favored stopover sites in Oregon include Youngs Bay, Nehalem Bay, Tillamook Bay, Yaquina Bay, and Coos Bay, where migrants and modest numbers of overwintering birds can be expected between October and May. Strays are occasionally found in Cackling Goose flocks in the Willamette Valley.

Adult. All black head, neck, and breast with a white collar across the upper throat. Black legs and bill. Juveniles have less white on the throat and conspicuous barring on wing coverts.

Cackling Goose

Branta hutchinsii

L 25" | **WS** 51"

Once considered a small form of the Canada Goose, the Cackling Goose is now recognized as a separate species. The wintering range has shifted north from the Sacramento Valley to Oregon's Willamette Valley, where large flocks now darken the skies between April and October. Cackling Geese vary widely in size and color; larger, paler individuals can be difficult to distinguish from Canadas. Cackling Geese give high-pitched yelping calls that are quite different from the harsh honking of Canada Geese.

Adult. Black head with flat crown and white "chinstrap." Short black bill and short neck.

Canada Goose

Branta canadensis

L 30-43" | **WS** 50-67"

Beginning in the late twentieth century, large Canada Geese from the Great Basin profited from intentional releases and habitat changes to become omnipresent in Oregon, where they have successfully colonized urban and suburban habitats closed to hunting, such as parks, golf courses, and mitigation wetlands. Native Canada Geese remain common breeders and wintering birds in their original range in the Harney, Summer Lake, Klamath, and Warner Basins. A threatened Arctic population, the Dusky Canada Goose, winters exclusively in northwest Oregon and part of southwest Washington, where federal refuges have been created for it; the total population has ranged between 7,000 and 15,000 birds in recent decades.

Adult. Large and long-necked, with a black head and neck and a distinctive white cheek. Dusky Canada Goose (not shown) smaller and shorter-billed and noticeably darker above and below than other Canada Geese. Numbered red neck collars aid in tracking this threatened population.

Trumpeter Swan

Cygnus buccinator

L 54–62" | **WS** 80"

The Trumpeter Swan, largest of all American waterfowl, was hunted to near extinction by the early twentieth century. Its subsequent recovery is a true conservation success story, and today small flocks can be found among the wintering Tundra Swans in the Willamette Valley. In the early 2000s, one flock of Trumpeters north of Corvallis increased to more than fifty birds. East of the Cascades, they are now found around Bend, Prineville, and Summer Lake. A small flock was transplanted to Malheur in the 1950s, and another group was released at Summer Lake in the 1990s. The raspy honks of this species sound as if they were coming from a plastic toy horn.

Adult. All white, with a long, graceful neck. Forehead feathering comes to a point. Bill is black with some pinkish red along the gape and no yellow. Bill and facial skin form an evenly tapered wedge that wraps around the eye. In direct comparison, noticeably larger than Tundra Swan.

Tundra Swan

Cygnus columbianus

L 47—58" | **WS** 61"

This, the default swan in Oregon, is a fairly common migrant east of the Cascades, with a few overwintering. Thousands stop over in the Klamath Basin in spring and fall, with peak numbers there in February and March. Smaller numbers pass through Lake and Harney Counties. In western Oregon, Tundras are scarce away from a few favored sites. Several thousand traditionally winter between Eugene and Albany, where they graze on cultivated fields. Several hundred more typically winter in the Tualatin Valley bottomlands, and they are readily found on Sauvie Island between November and March. The call is a low-pitched, bugling *hoo oo hoo*.

Adult. Base of the bill straighter and more vertical than in Trumpeter. Black facial skin pinched and narrow where it meets the eye. Forehead feathering U-shaped, not pointed. The yellow spot on bill varies from absent to roughly the size of a thumbprint.

Wood Duck

Aix sponsa

L 20" | **WS** 27"

The striking male Wood Duck looks like an artist's hand-painted creation. The female shows stunning, ever changing patterns of subtle iridescence. Wood Ducks are retiring, mostly lurking in heavily wooded back channels, sloughs, and swamps. They are common to uncommon throughout western Oregon, where they use nest in natural cavities and manmade boxes. Wood Ducks have a taste for hazelnuts, and are sometimes found by the hundreds in Willamette Valley orchards. They are uncommon to rare east of the Cascades, where they are confined to lowland river valleys. The high-pitched, upslurred whistled *zeet* of the male is distinctive, while the female gives a succession of lower-pitched, squeaky *oo-week* calls.

Male. Smaller than a Mallard. Instantly recognizable, with long crest and dazzling mix of colors and white stripes. Bill is red, white, and black.

Female. Mostly dark brown and gray with pale spotting on breast and flanks. Crest shorter than the male's. White in the face is restricted to a large football-shaped patch around the eye.

Gadwall
Mareca strepera

L 20" | **WS** 33"

Aside from the Mallard, Gadwall is the most widespread breeding duck in Oregon. Like other dabblers, Gadwalls feed by sifting food from the water surface or by tipping up to probe the muddy shallows. They habitually hold their bill pointed downward at a 45-degree angle, while other dabblers present a more horizontal profile. The creation of small mitigation wetlands and larger refuge complexes has benefited this year-round resident greatly. Gadwalls used to nest only east of the Cascades, but in the early 2000s, they started breeding in the Willamette Valley and coastal valleys, where they are now common in summer. The male's call is a soft, nasal, burping *quack*.

Male. At a distance, entirely gray with black undertail and a white patch in the wing. Up close, the finely vermiculated body plumage is stunning. Variable head pattern, with more contrast between the crown and face in some birds. Legs and feet yellow, bill all black.

Female. Strongly mottled dark brown and buffy. White wing patch often exposed. Face paler than that of a female Mallard, with a less conspicuous dark eye stripe; smaller bill is yellow-orange on the sides and dark down the middle.

Mallard

Anas platyrhynchos

L 23" | **WS** 35"

Familiar to nearly every Oregonian, the Mallard, or "Green-head," is a readily found resident throughout the state. Mallards are habitat generalists, found almost anywhere there is water, from modest drainage ditches to expansive coastal estuaries and even high mountain lakes. Like most dabblers, Mallards are ground nesters, typically hiding their nests in dense pond-side vegetation. In the summer, males transition into a cryptic, female-like plumage referred to as "eclipse," making them less conspicuous during a molting period that renders them temporarily flightless. The female's simple loud quack call is the "sound a duck makes" learned by all children.

Male. Easily recognized by its bright green head, pale gray body, dark chestnut-brown breast, and white neck ring. Bill uniformly greenish yellow. Bright orange legs and feet.

Female. Uniformly mottled warm brown. Head paler tan, with a dark brown crown and stripe from the base of the bill through the eye. Mostly orange bill.

American Wigeon

Anas americana

L 20" | **WS** 32"

This species is among the most abundant wintering ducks in Oregon, particularly along the outer coast, where wet dairy pastures and estuary shallows provide ample habitat for grazing. Grassy parks with duck ponds and golf courses offer attractive urban and suburban wintering habitats for wigeon. Since they don't typically sift food from the water surface, wigeons' pale bluish bills are smaller and much narrower than those of other dabbling ducks. Small numbers of American Wigeon summer in Oregon, with a few breeding, but September to April is the best time to find them in large, constantly moving, tight-knit flocks. The male's hollow whistled call is a distinctive, slightly down-slurred *hee-hoo*.

Male. Body mostly pinkish brown, with large white patch on lower flanks and black undertail. Head is pale gray to gray-brown, with a white crown stripe and broad iridescent green stripe. Bill is pale blue.

Female. Uniformly warm brown on breast and flanks, with mottled gray-brown lower flanks. Bill is mostly bluish.

Eurasian Wigeon

Anas penelope

L 16.5-20.5" | **WS** 31"

This Old World duck is a regular wintering species along the Pacific Coast of North America, where it can be found in the company of large flocks of American Wigeon. Eurasians are generally rare east of the Cascades, except for in the Klamath Basin. Females are virtually identical to their American counterparts, but are more reddish brown on head. Wigeon are mostly grazers, typically feeding on short grass pastures, grassy parks with duck ponds, and golf courses. Males give a loud, up-slurred whistled *sweee* that rings out above the two-noted whistles of Americans.

Male. Easily separated from male American Wigeon by its mostly gray body and rich cinnamon head. Crown stripe cream-colored; often lacks green head stripe shown by American. Bill is mostly pale blue with a black tip.

Female. Nearly identical to a female American Wigeon, but with a warmer reddish brown head.

Blue-winged Teal
Spatula discors

L 15" | **WS** 23"

Blue-winged Teal, one of three Oregon ducks with light blue
wing patches, are late spring migrants, typically not appearing
in Oregon before the last days of April. They nest commonly
in the larger freshwater marshes east of the Cascades, and are
locally uncommon breeders on the westside. They prefer large
shallow wetlands and marshes with extensive reed beds or deep
grass. Like other teal, they are faster fliers than larger dabbling
ducks. Their understated nasal quacks and soft hollow whistles
are not often heard.

Male. Conspicuous white
face crescent on a small,
dark gray-brown duck
unique. Light blue wing
patch easily seen in flight.

Female. Smaller than most
dabbling ducks, with paler
and grayer face than
female Cinnamon Teal.

Cinnamon Teal

Spatula cyanoptera

L 14-17" | **WS** 25"

No duck better deserves its name than the male Cinnamon Teal. This species is most often found on freshwater marshes, small ponds, and seasonal wetlands with deep grass and reeds. Cinnamon Teal breed abundantly in the expansive marshy basins east of the Cascades, especially at Malheur NWR and in the Klamath Basin. They nest less commonly in wetlands on the state's westside. Although small numbers overwinter in western Oregon, Cinnamon Teal are more readily found in Oregon from April to early October.

Male. Entirely reddish brown, with iridescent shimmer in bright sunlight. Bill longer and a bit more spoon-shaped than in Blue-winged Teal.

Female. Nearly identical to female Blue-winged, but warmer brown overall; face paler and pale area at the base of the bill more diffuse, not forming a well-defined spot.

Northern Shoveler
Spatula clypeata

L 19" | **WS** 30"

The distinctive long, spoon-shaped bill is used to strain food items off the water surface as the bird paddles along with neck and bill outstretched. Shovelers favor sewage ponds, where they often gather around inflow pipes in swirling feeding scrums of a hundred or more, grunting and quaking nasally. They are uncommon breeders at marshes and wetlands in Oregon, but common to abundant statewide in spring and fall. They are common in winter west of the Cascades. Dabbler flocks in the Willamette Valley and flooded coastal pastures are sure to have good numbers of shovelers.

Male. Dark green head, with white breast and reddish brown flanks; yellow eye. Bill disproportionately long and broad at the tip.

Female. Suggestive of female Mallard, but rides lower in the water; shorter neck and longer, more clearly spoon-shaped bill.

Northern Pintail

Anas acuta

L 25" | **WS** 34"

One of western Oregon's most abundant wintering ducks. Migrants pack coastal estuaries by the thousands in August and September. As winter approaches, they move into semi-flooded dairy pastures, corn stubble, seasonal wetlands, and the sodden fields of the Willamette Valley. The long, thin neck, pointed wings, and attenuated tail make the sleek and graceful Northern Pintail one of the easiest ducks to identify in flight. Tens of thousands pass through the Klamath Basin between February and April. Pintails rarely nest or summer west of the Cascades, but are uncommon breeders in marshlands east of the Cascades. The most commonly heard call is a single hollow whistle.

Male. Chocolate-brown head, white breast, gray flanks, and long pointed tail. White stripe from the breast tapers as it extends up the side of the neck onto the back of the head. Slender bill is mostly pale blue with black on the top and at the base.

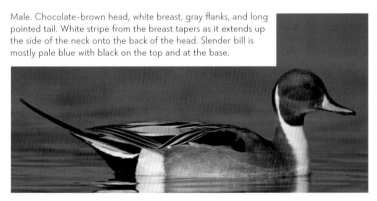

Female. Sleeker and longer-necked than other dabblers. Body mottled, warmer and buffier than other female ducks. Face unmarked tawny.

Green-winged Teal

Anas carolinensis

L 14" | **WS** 23"

This duck is the smallest dabbler in North America, a fast and direct flier so tiny that it can even be mistaken for a sandpiper at a distance. Green-winged Teal are common migrants and abundant winterers in Oregon, found in habitats from the shallows of coastal estuaries to seasonally flooded pastures and small ponds. They feed mostly on exposed mudflats, typically spreading out into easily distinguished male/female pairs. Green-winged Teal are very sparse breeders in Oregon, but from late August through April they are common to abundant in appropriate habitats. Their high-pitched, slightly trilled whistles can be heard from many hundreds of yards away.

Male. Mostly gray body with dark reddish brown head and iridescent green eye stripe. Vertical white stripe between breast and flanks.

Female. Very small mottled brown duck with an all-dark bill. Typically keeps close company with the more easily recognized male.

Canvasback
Aythya valisineria

L 21" | **WS** 33"

Canvasbacks breed uncommonly in the marsh complexes east of the Cascades, and are generally sparse in migration and winter across most of Oregon. Spring migrants are abundant in the Klamath Basin from February to April, particularly on Upper Klamath and the ponds along Stateline Road. Smaller numbers migrate through the Harney and Lake County Basins. Canvasbacks prefer larger lakes, reservoirs, and coastal bays.

Male. Large diving duck best identified by its angular head shape. Dark ski-slope bill and forehead with a peaked hind crown. Looks white-bodied at a distance. Head dark cinnamon-brown.

Females and immatures darker gray to gray-brown, with washed-out brown heads. Ski-slope bill all dark.

Redhead
Aythya americana

L 19" | **WS** 29"

The Redhead is Oregon's most abundant breeding diving duck, nesting commonly in marshes east of the Cascades; since 2000, the breeding range has expanded to several sites west of the Cascades, most notably Fern Ridge Reservoir near Eugene. Redheads nest in dense cattails and reeds. They are abundant migrants east of the Cascades, particularly on the Klamath, Lake, and Harney County basins. A few winter west of the Cascades.

Male. Rich reddish brown rounded head. Medium-gray body with a solid black breast. Bill is pale grayish blue, crossed by whitish band and black tip.

Female. Drab and uniformly warm earthy brown. Dark-tipped bill darker bluish gray than male's, lacks conspicuous whitish band. Steeper forehead and rounder crown than similar female Canvasback.

Ring-necked Duck

Aythya collaris

L 17" | **WS** 25"

Scarce nesters in Oregon, Ring-necked Ducks are uncommon to common outside of the breeding season. From October to April, good numbers can be found on flooded pastures along the coast, sewage treatment ponds, and the seasonally inundated bottomlands of western Oregon's interior. The nasal grunting quack is rarely heard.

Male. Squared-off crown and a solid black back. Sides are dark gray separated from the black breast by a contrasting pale, almost white wedge. Distinctive mostly dark gray-blue bill is framed by white at the base and in front of the black tip.

Female. Scaup-like, but has much paler face, with extensive pale feathering at the base of the bill, white eye ring, and short pale stripe behind the eye. Bill pattern more subtle than the male's, without white base.

Greater Scaup

Aythya marila

L 18" | **WS** 28"

The larger of the two scaup, Greaters are mostly coastal migrants, preferring estuaries, large lakes, and reservoirs. Tens of thousands winter along the Columbia River, where they feed on invasive mussels. Feeding flocks often include both scaup species, a good opportunity to compare size and head shapes side by side. They don't often vocalize away from breeding grounds.

Male. Pale gray to white flanks, with darker gray back and black breast and undertail. Head often shows dark green iridescence. Bill almost entirely bluish gray, with a fairly broad black nail. Peaked fore crown and more rounded profile separate males from the similar Lesser Scaup.

Female. Virtually identical to female Lesser Scaup, but note different head shape. Extensive white feathering at the base of the bill. Often shows a weak pale crescent on the lower cheek behind the eye, a mark not seen on female Lesser Scaup.

Lesser Scaup

Aythya affinis

L 16" | **WS** 29"

Lesser Scaup are inconspicuous migrants throughout Oregon, typically found in groups of fifty or less. They tend to avoid marine waters and larger lakes, favoring smaller bodies of water such as urban duck ponds and sewage treatment impoundments. Like Greater Scaup, they have shifted their winter range to feast on the invasive bi-valves in the Columbia River, where they can be found in rafts numbering into the hundreds. Lesser is a scarce breeder in Oregon.

Male. Nearly identical to male Greater Scaup, but distinguished by peaked hind crown. In flight, white wing stripe in the wing is restricted to the secondaries and does not extend into the outer flight feathers.

Female. Virtually identical to female Greater Scaup, but more squared off hind crown and smaller bill. Less extensive white feathering around the base of the bill. Lacks diffuse white crescent on lower cheek.

Harlequin Duck

Histrionicus histrionicus

L 17" | **WS** 22-26"

In appearance and behavior, few ducks rival the Harlequin. Harlequins bob and dive in the turbulent surf as it pounds basalt outcroppings, somehow managing not to get smashed into the rocks. They are mostly coastal denizens, found near sea stacks, rocky shorelines, and jetties. The south jetty in Newport's Yaquina Bay is a reliable place to see this bird at close range. During the breeding season, Harlequins withdraw inland and become quite secretive, nesting along the heavily wooded banks of fast-moving mountain rivers and streams.

Male. Looks hand-painted, with striking patches of white interrupting their steely blue and chestnut plumage.

Female. Uniformly sooty-brown, with a neat white spot behind the eye and diffuse whitish crescent at the base of the bill.

Surf Scoter
Melanitta perspicillata

L 23" | **WS** 30"

Scoters are heavy blackish sea ducks, typically seen in flocks just beyond the breakers. The Surf Scoter is the most frequently encountered in Oregon. Found along the outer coast throughout the year, this species does not nest in the state, but thousands winter along the coast. They also inhabit coastal inlets and estuaries, and sometimes winter inland along the Columbia, where they feed on invasive mussels. During October and November, small numbers of Surf Scoters pass through the interior, making rest stops on large lakes and reservoirs and along the Columbia River. Wintering flocks sometimes segregate by sex.

Male. All black, with white on the back of the head. Spectacular multicolored bill is the most prominent feature.

Female. Sooty gray-brown females and immatures have two pale patches on the face. Bill structurally similar to male's but all dark.

White-winged Scoter

Melanitta fusca

L 21" | **WS** 31"

In Oregon, North America's largest scoter is generally restricted to the outer coast, where it is found on the open ocean just beyond the surf and in the lower reaches of estuaries. At the height of spring and fall migration, White-wingeds may be as numerous as Surf Scoters, but they are far less common in midwinter. They are often found in mixed flocks with Surf and Black Scoters. Inland strays are found annually from October to December, mostly along the Columbia River or on large lakes and reservoirs in the Cascades. This arctic nester is typically absent from the from June to August.

Male. All black, often showing a large patch of white in the folded wing and a distinctive white comma-shaped mark below the eye. Bill knob is black, with the lower part and tip of the bill a mix of orange, red, and white.

Female. Very similar to female Surf Scoter, with two whitish facial patches and a thick, all-dark wedge-shaped bill. White wing patch, absent in Surf Scoter, is typically visible on the water and always conspicuous in flight.

Black Scoter
Melanitta americana

L 19" | **WS** 33"

The Black Scoter is less abundant in Oregon than the larger Surf and White-winged Scoters. It can be hard to find away from such favored sites as the beach north of Yaquina Head in Lincoln County and off the Nelscott area at the south end of Lincoln City. Cape Arago in Coos County and the rockier shores in northern Lane County also host sizable wintering flocks. Black Scoters tend to feed near shore, often in surf between the breakers and the beach. They are rare inland in Oregon. Unlike other scoters, which don't usually vocalize away from the breeding grounds, male Black Scoters in winter frequently throw their heads back to give a mournful, down-slurred whistling call.

Male. All black, with a more rounded, domed head than other scoters. Bill is smaller, with a conspicuous orangish yellow knob at the base.

Female. Dark chocolate-brown body. Head pattern quite different from other Oregon scoters, pale gray on the cheek and upper neck contrasting with the dark dusky brown crown and nape.

Bufflehead

Bucephala albeola

L 13" | **WS** 21"

North America's smallest diving duck is readily found in Oregon outside of the nesting season. Buffleheads are common to abundant statewide from October to April, but they only rarely breed in the state. They use almost any body of water, from small farm ponds and flooded fields to the largest lakes, reservoirs, and bays, but avoid the open ocean. Feeding birds dive frenetically; at the start of the breeding season, males chase females. Flight is fast and direct, with very rapid wingbeats.

Male. Striking white and black pattern conspicuous and distinctive even at a distance.

Female. Uniformly dusky, with a distinctive grayish white patch on the cheek. Stubby triangular bill.

Common Goldeneye
Bucephala clangula

L 24" | **WS** 33"

The Common Goldeneye winters on Oregon's major rivers, large lakes and reservoirs, and coastal bays from October to April. This species is most readily found on estuaries and along the entire length of the Columbia River; flocks are usually small, but sometimes up to several dozen join to form a raft. In flight, the wings produce a loud staccato whistle. Deep divers, Common Goldeneye use their short, powerful triangular bills to dislodge bivalves and other prey. These cavity nesters occasionally breed at montane lakes in far northeastern Oregon.

Male. Mostly white, with a black head (iridescent green in bright sun) and back and a distinctive round white patch between the bright yellow eye and the base of the bill.

Female. Gray body with white in folded wings and dark cinnamon-brown head. White collar between the head and breast. Peaked mid-crown. May have some yellow on triangular bill, which is slightly longer than its height. Yellow eye.

Barrow's Goldeneye

Bucephala islandica

L 17–19" | **WS** 28.25"

Very similar to the more abundant and widespread Common, Barrow's Goldeneyes are rare winterers on the coastal bays where Common Goldeneyes are most abundant, but wintering populations of Barrow's are increasing along the Columbia River, where the two species can often be seen side by side. Flocks of Barrow's can also be found at the outflows of large reservoirs in the Cascades; Foster Reservoir near Sweet Home is a reliable site. Cavity nesters like the Common Goldeneye, Barrow's breed at several high lakes in the Cascades, Blue, and Wallowa Mountains . Their wings produce a staccato whistle in flight.

Male. Crescent-shaped face patch and extensive black on the back, extending as a spur onto the breast side.

Female. Steeply sloped forehead and peaked forecrown. Small bill often shows extensive orangish yellow.

Hooded Merganser

Lophodytes cucullatus

L 18" | **WS** 24"

By far the smallest of Oregon's three merganser species, the secretive Hooded Merganser prefers heavily wooded ponds, sloughs, and back channels. Hooded Mergansers are incredibly fast fliers, with rapid, shallow wingbeats. They winter state-wide, but are more common as breeders west of the Cascades. Unlike other diving ducks and mergansers, this species does not form large flocks.

Male. Unique angular head shape with black and white crest. White head patch might lead to confusion with male Bufflehead, but white does not wrap across nape. White breast, warm brown flanks. Black back and vertical stripes on upper flanks. Bill is flat and thin, with slight hook at tip.

Female. Same head shape as male, but body entirely gray to gray-brown; head is warm reddish brown.

Common Merganser

Mergus merganser

L 25" | **WS** 34"

This large, thin-billed duck has an elongated, loon-like profile. Common Mergansers retire to smaller streams during the nesting season, but over the rest of the year they are found primarily on larger bodies of freshwater, tending to avoid salt and brackish waters. They often form large feeding flocks that dive and work cooperatively to herd schools of small fish into shallows. Common Mergansers nest throughout Oregon, most often along the small fast-moving tributaries of larger rivers.

Male. Mostly white with a dark green head (looks black at a distance) and bright red bill.

Female. Medium-gray body with pale gray to whitish breast; warm cinnamon-brown head may show a slight crest. Crisp demarcation between head and breast.

Red-breasted Merganser

Mergus serrator

L 27" | **WS** 30"

Slightly smaller than the Common Merganser, this species does not breed in Oregon, but winters commonly in the state from October to April, almost exclusively on saltwater and the brackish water of coastal estuaries. Red-breasted Mergansers seem to prefer shallower bays with sandy substrates, where they tend to feed along the main channels on the incoming and outgoing tides. Siletz Bay and Netarts Bay are reliable sites. They are rare inland in spring and fall migration.

Male. Shape and structure similar to the larger, bulkier Common Merganser, but more colorful and strikingly patterned. Heavily-spotted reddish-brown breast. Gray and white flanks and black back. Longer, wispier crest.

Female. Slightly smaller, but otherwise similar to female Common Merganser. Head paler and less cinnamon than Common's, with less contrast between the head and dingy buffy grayish breast.

Ruddy Duck

Oxyura jamaicensis

L 15" | **WS** 23"

This small diver has an oversized head and bill relative to its body size. During winter and migration, Ruddy Ducks inhabit small ponds, lakes, protected bays, and other placid waters. They nest in expansive freshwater marshes, typically around cattails. The male's animated courtship display includes rapid head bobbing while the bill is vigorously drummed against the breast. Some winter east of the Cascades, mostly in sheltered coves along the Columbia River. In western Oregon, migrant and wintering flocks can be expected at most sewage ponds and larger wetland complexes. Tualatin River National Wildlife Refuge and the Sheridan sewage ponds often host large wintering flocks.

Male. Breeding adult has rich chestnut-brown body, white cheeks, and black cap accentuated by a stunning baby-blue bill. At other seasons the bill is dusky blue-gray, and the body plumage is dull brown.

Females. Mostly mottled brown, with distinctive dark stripes running across the pale face. Bill all dark year-round.

Mountain Quail

Oreortyx pictus

L 10.25-12.25" | **WS** 14-16"

Though common in appropriate habitats, this secretive denizen of brush-covered montane slopes is the nemesis bird of many birders, rarely giving more than a fleeting glimpse before flushing or scurrying off into impenetrable vegetation. Mountain Quail ar resident in all of Oregon's mountain ranges, at elevations generally between 1500 and 5000 feet. They prefer natural forest openings and early successional growth in recent clearcuts. Slowly driving logging roads or walking old clearcuts offers the best chance of finding this species. Family groups of Mountain Quail forage for grit along road edges and in disturbed openings. Territorial males perch on rocks or large stumps when issuing their loud, hollow *qweeark* calls. Also listen for soft clucking "rally" calls used to alert other quail to threats.

Adult. Mostly medium-gray and olive-brown above. Throat and belly are rich chestnut, with white hash markings along flanks. Two long, straight crown plumes, with no expansion at tip, generally lie back, but stand straight up when the bird is alarmed.

California Quail
Callipepla californica

L 9.5–10.5" | **WS** 12.5–14.5"

Most quail seen in Oregon are of this species, colloquially referred to as the "Valley Quail." Uncommon to abundant throughout the inland valleys west of the Cascades, but absent from the outer coast except in southern Coos and Curry Counties. Readily found in open and semi-open habitats east of the Cascades. During winter, eastside populations often move into semi-urban areas and small towns, sometimes by the hundreds. Almost any kind of cover can serve as a nest site, including brush piles, blackberry mounds, and dense hedgerows. Quail sometimes come to bird feeders in suburban and rural areas. The most common vocalization is a slurred three-noted *Chi cah go*.

Male. Mostly gray and olive-brown above, with a buffy, scaly looking belly with oval chestnut patch. Rich chestnut flanks with white streaks. Black face surrounded by white. Forward-curving topknot feathers have bulbous tip.

Female. Mostly gray and olive-brown body. Less patterned than male. Extremely short topknot feathers; no black in the face or chestnut on pale scaly belly. Immature much like adult female.

Chukar
Alectoris chukar

L 13.25-15" | **WS** 31"

This Old World partridge was widely introduced across the American West during the mid-twentieth century. Since the first successful release in the state in 1951, Chukars have spread into the basalt rimrocks and rocky slopes throughout the basin and range country of southeastern Oregon. Chukars run almost as fast as they fly, rarely flushing like other upland game birds. When you think you have them pinned down, they are usually walking up a hillside 200 yards away. Males often perch on a large boulder or rimrock precipice as they belt out their *chucka, chucka, chucka, chucka* territorial calls.

Adult. Sexes similar. Mostly gray and buffy pinkish brown, with a piano key-like black and white pattern on flanks. Face and throat white surrounded by broad black border. Bright red bill and eye ring, thick reddish legs and feet.

Ring-necked Pheasant

Phasianus colchicus

L 20-28 | **WS** 22-34"

Oregon introductions of this non-native game bird date back to the late nineteenth century, and continue today. Supplemental releases for hunting season may be all that sustains pheasants in some areas, as modern agriculture practices have stripped away much of the hedgerow cover they need for breeding and protection, causing once sturdy populations to decline or disappear. Pheasants still thrive in the Klamath and other less cultivated basins and plateaus in eastern Oregon. The male's call is a grating series of metallic croaks, given in stuttering two-note phrases.

Male. Dark green head with red wattle surrounding the eye and a corn-yellow bill. Body a scaly-looking mix of golden rust and chestnut-brown. Long tail feathers are brown with black barring.

Female. Cryptic; mostly pale buffy brown with dark mottling. Tail feathers taper like male's but not as long.

Ruffed Grouse

Bonasa umbellus

L 15—19 | **WS** 20—25"

Oregon's most widespread grouse is named for the ruff of neck and shoulder feathers raised by displaying males. Though infrequently encountered, Ruffed Grouse are fairly numerous in most of Oregon's mountain ranges. They are ground dwellers, favoring dense, moist streamside underbrush and heavily vegetated coastal bogs and riparian lowlands. They are often found gathering grit along gravel logging roads in the Cascades and Coast Ranges. Standing atop a favored drumming log, displaying males fan their tail feathers like a turkey and beat their wings against their breasts to produce a low-pitched series that accelerates into a high-speed crescendo. Vocalizations are soft clucking contact calls.

Male. Heavily mottled. Coastal and lowland populations tend to be more reddish brown, while interior and higher-elevation populations are grayer overall. Crown is slightly crested. Female similar to male, but more cryptic and duller in color. Not distinctly crested.

Greater Sage Grouse

Centrocercus urophasianus

L 22-29.5 | **WS** 31 "

Our largest grouse is an iconic symbol of the vast swaths of sagebrush that formerly covered much of the American West. Courtship occurs at leks, where dozens of males gather to compete for female attention, fanning their spiky tail feathers, strutting, and producing an odd set of bubbling sounds by inflating air sacs on their breast. This unique display is no longer common in their southeastern Oregon haunts: many leks have gone quiet, and others have only a couple displaying males. These dramatic population declines are generally attributed to overgrazing and conversion to agriculture, resulting in habitat loss and fragmentation across much of the former range; hunting pressure has also played a role.

Male (above). Large chicken-like bird with long, spiked tail feathers. Black on the throat and upper breast and belly, with a scarf-like wrap of fluffy white feathers around the neck and sides of the breast. Female (right). Considerably smaller than the male. Cryptic gray-brown overall, with black on the lower belly. Pointed tail feathers not as long as male's.

Dusky Grouse
Dendragapus obscurus

Sooty Grouse
Dendragapus fuliginosus

L 15.75-20 | **WS** 24-28"

These two high-elevation residents are nearly identical and were formerly considered the same species. Both are normally found above 2500 feet in elevation, all the way up to timberline. They can be comically approachable, whence the colloquial name "fool hen." The Sooty Grouse is the coastal species, inhabiting the wetter slopes of the Coast Range, Siskiyou Mountains, and the Cascades. Dusky Grouse are found in the Ochoco, Blue, and Wallowa Mountains. The courtship "hooting" of both species is a series of low-pitched *woops* produced by the male's air sacs. Male Sooty Grouse typically conceal themselves high in conifers and walk back and forth on a branch as they give usually six loud hoots, while Dusky Grouse issue usually five very soft, extremely low-pitched notes from the ground.

Male Dusky (above). Bare skin on neck is dark reddish purple. Slightly paler, with more whitish mottling than Sooty Grouse. Almost completely black tail lacks the obvious gray band shown by Sooty Grouse. Male Sooty (right). Bare skin on neck is yellowish. Slightly darker, with less white on flanks than Dusky. Broad pale gray band on tip of otherwise blackish tail.

Wild Turkey

Meleagris gallopavo

L 37–46" | **WS** 50–64"

All Wild Turkeys in Oregon are the descendants of birds introduced from Texas and the eastern United States. They are now
numerous in the foothills of the Rogue, Umpqua, and southern
Willamette Valleys, but scarce east of the Cascades, where they
are mostly restricted to lowland valleys in the Ochoco, Blue,
and Wallowa Mountains and the foothills of the Cascades;
essentially absent from southeast Oregon. Turkeys favor dry
slopes with a mix of conifers, oaks, and madrone and a sparse
understory. Hormone-charged males will gobble in response to
almost any loud sound, including the slam of a car door.

Adult. Easily recognized
by very large size, long
sturdy legs, and
featherless gray to
light blue heads. Adult
male has distinctive red
wattle hanging down
from the throat.

Pied-billed Grebe

Podilymbus podiceps

L 13" | **WS** 21"

This small, tailless duck-like bird is a year-round resident statewide, inhabiting all types of water bodies except for open ocean. Grebes rarely fly, and getting airborne always appears to be a challenge as they run clumsily across the surface of the water while frantically beating their stubby wings. Landings are no more graceful. They dive for food, and submerge when threatened, often leaving only the head and part of the neck above the surface. Pied-billed Grebes nest on floating platforms of marsh vegetation. Like other grebes, their tiny stripe-faced offspring ride on the backs of their parents until they are about half grown. The call is a whooping series of how-ow, how-ow, how-ow notes.

Breeding adult. Uniformly dark dusky brown with a fluffy whitish cotton ball-like rump. Thick stubby bill is pale silvery gray with a single black vertical stripe. Complete white eye ring.

Winter adult/ immature. Pale whitish throat and warm reddish brown foreneck and breast. Bill dull yellowish horn-colored.

Red-necked Grebe

Podiceps grisegena

L 17—22 | **WS** 21—22"

This large, thick-necked grebe is a decided loner, rarely seen in groups of more than two or three individuals. Red-necked Grebes winter uncommonly all along the Oregon coast, where they can be seen from September to April feeding beyond the breakers on the open ocean or in the lower reaches of estuaries at the incoming and outgoing tide. Between the jetties at Yaquina and Tillamook Bays are among the more reliable places to find this species. Upper Klamath Lake is the only place in Oregon where Red-necked Grebes have consistently nested.

Breeding adult. Large, triangular head with flat crown. Long, stout, dagger-like bill straw- to corn- yellow with dark upper ridge. Blackish crown, white cheek, rich chestnut foreneck and dusky brown back.

Non-breeding/ immature. Mostly dusky brown above, with dingy pale cheek and warm brown to dingy gray foreneck.

Horned Grebe

Podiceps auritus

L 14 " | **WS** 23 "

This highly migratory grebe, which breeds mostly north of
Oregon, is easily found on the outer coast from October to
April. Sometimes seen in small flocks during migration. Horned
Grebes prefer large open expanses of water, including the open
ocean and bays, and also winter fairly commonly along the
Columbia River and on a few larger reservoirs; they are other-
wise scarce inland. A few pairs breed at Malheur N.W.R. and
in the Klamath Basin, where they are far outnumbered by
Eared Grebes.

Breeding adult. Mostly black head and back, with rich chestnut foreneck, breast, and flanks. Wispy golden orange crests on sides of head. Bright red eye and small, dagger-like dark bill with a fine ivory tip.

Non-breeding/immature. Bicolored, with dusky gray brown crown, hind neck, and back, and whitish to dingy pale gray face, foreneck, and underparts. Flat, anvil-like crown, thicker neck, and fine pale tip on bill distinguish this species from the very similar Eared Grebe in all plumages.

Eared Grebe

Podiceps nigricollis

L 12—14 | **WS** 21—22"

Although easily confused with the Horned Grebe, this species represents the inverse in terms of habitat choice and seasonality. Eared Grebes are common to abundant breeders at most inland marsh complexes east of the Cascades, but are generally scarce on the outer coast at any season. Only a few Eared Grebes winter in Oregon, mostly on a few sewage ponds in the Willamette Valley and occasionally in coastal estuaries. They are sparse migrants along the outer coast, instead passing through the interior, where southbound migrants gather by thousands in late July and August at Abert Lake in Lake County to feast on brine flies and their larvae.

Breeding adult. Mostly black head, neck, and back, with rich chestnut flanks. Bright red eye. Short thin bill looks slightly upturned.

Non-breeding/ immature. Dusky gray brown above, dingy gray brown below. Peaked forecrown and thinner neck, along with lack of pale bill tip, separate Eared from very similar Horned Grebe. Neck angled forward when swimming. Fluffier rump than Horned.

Western Grebe

Aechmophorus occidentalis

L 21-29 | **WS** 31—33"

The unforgettable courtship dance of this graceful species, when two birds run side by side across the water, has appeared in many nature shows, making the Western Grebe a favorite among the many striking birds of freshwater marshes in the American West. Fuzzy young routinely ride on their parents' backs until about half-grown. Western Grebes nest commonly throughout the basin and range country of southeastern Oregon, and are abundant breeders at Fern Ridge Reservoir west of Eugene. Most retreat to the outer coast in winter, where large rafts can be seen resting just offshore; they also winter commonly on and at several large reservoirs west of the Cascades Though generally absent east of the Cascades from December to February, numbers winter on pools behind the dams on the Columbia River.

Adult. Large, with long thin neck. Long bill is straw-greenish to dull corn-yellow, with dark upper ridge. Distinctly bicolored plumage, dusky gray to blackish above and clean white below. Dark facial feathering completely surrounds the bright red eye.

Clark's Grebe

Aechmophorus clarkii

L 21-29 | **WS** 32"

At Malheur N.W.R. and other southeastern Oregon marshes, breeding Clark's and Western Grebes occur in nearly equal numbers, while Westerns outnumber Clark's about five to one at Fern Ridge Reservoir, the only nesting site for either species west of the Cascades. Hardly any Clark's Grebes winter in Oregon.

Adult. Virtually identical to Western Grebe. Looks paler overall from a distance, with more white and light gray on flanks. Eye completely surrounded by white feathers. Narrower band of dark down hindneck. Brighter yellow-orange bill, with limited dark on upper ridge.

Rock Pigeon

Columba livia

L 11.5–14" | **WS** 19.75–26.5"

This non-native bird has thrived since coming to North America with some of the earliest European settlers. Rock Pigeons are ubiquitous in highly urbanized areas, where tall man-made structures such as buildings and bridges mimic the cliff faces and rocky outcroppings used for nesting and roost sites in their home range. Owyhee Canyon and Succor Creek Canyon in far eastern Oregon and many of the steep basalt cliffs in the Columbia River Gorge offer opportunities to see hundreds of these birds in traditional cliff habitats. Captive breeding and frequent escapes supplement wild populations and account for the wide variety of color patterns seen in free-flying flocks. They are powerful fliers often used for racing and homing competitions. Call is a rough, throaty cooing.

Adult. Mostly pale gray. Head darker purplish gray. Neck and breast a mix of green and purplish iridescence. Reddish pink feet. Many color variants, most of which show extensive white and browns.

Band-tailed Pigeon

Patagioenas fasciata

L 13-16" | **WS** 25"

Unlike the more abundant feral Rock Pigeon, Oregon's largest
native pigeon tends to be found in heavily forested areas away
from human habitation. In flight, the Band-tailed Pigeon's
longer tail and distinctive shallow fluttering wingbeats allow
it to be identified at great distances. This canopy- dwelling
species breeds commonly in moist mid- to low-elevation conifer
forests of the Coast Range, Siskiyou Mountains, and western
slopes of the Cascades. It is generally rare anywhere east of the
Cascades. Only a few winter in Oregon. Spring migrants arrive
in March, and most depart by the end of September. Extremely
low-pitched song is a series of hiccuping hoots.

Adult. Longer-tailed than Rock Pigeons. Fairly uniform greenish-gray above and brownish
to pinkish-gray below. Distinctive white half-collar on nape borders greenish iridescence
on the lower hind neck. Tail mostly gray, with blackish band and broad pale gray to
whitish tip. Bill yellow with black tip.

Eurasian Collared-Dove

Streptopelia decaocto

L 11.5-11.75" | **WS** 18.5-21.5"

The statewide population of this non-native newcomer has exploded since these large doves first appeared in Oregon about two decades ago. They are now common to abundant residents in and around small and mid-sized towns all over the state. Large flocks are often found near farms and grain elevators, where spilled grain provides a stable food supply. They have also moved into suburban and semi-urban habitats, but they have yet to populate heavily urbanized parts of the Portland Metro area. Can breed at any season, typically nesting in the dense foliage of ornamental spruces and cedars. Hollow, three-note *koo-koo kook* song is often repeated.

Adult. Overall color suggests a heavily creamed latte, with black semi-collar at the base of the hind neck. Darker brown to blackish outer flight feathers. Lacks iridescence and scaly patterns seen on other doves and pigeons. Dark base to the undertail. All-black bill and dark pinkish red feet and legs.

Mourning Dove

Zenaida macroura

L 12" **WS** 16"

A habitat generalist, this dove is readily found in most open and semi-open sub-montane habitats, except along the northern coast, where it is generally absent. Greatest abundance is in open farmlands dominated by grain and hay crops like wheat and alfalfa. Mourning Doves are known to breed in every month of the year even at colder latitudes, typically laying two eggs in famously flimsy nests. Frequent visitor to urban and suburban bird feeders, especially in winter. Song a soft, mournful *who-oo, hoo, hoo, hoo.*

Adult. Tail long and tapered, unlike other Oregon doves and pigeons. Pale sandy brown overall, with dark spotting on wings. Pinkish breast. Plain face accentuated by large dark eye with light blue ring. Comparatively short, thin black bill with pinkish red gape. Limited iridescence on nape.

Common Nighthawk

Chordeiles minor

L 9" | **WS** 22.5"

Nighthawks arrive in Oregon late in spring, typically after Memorial Day. They are most abundant in arid climates, particularly the pine forests and high desert steppes east of the Cascades. They are less common in western Oregon, where they are found mostly in foothill and mid-elevation mountain habitats with openings and clearcuts. During the day, nighthawks roost on rooftops, horizontal tree limbs, and even fence rails. They nest on the ground, atop gravel or leaf litter, and sometimes on gravel rooftops in urban areas. A strongly nasal *peeent* is their only vocalization. The wings of males also produce a loud whirring *vvvvveeer* in their steep display dives.

Adult. Broad white bars across pointed wings is the one obvious field mark on the otherwise cryptic plumage. When roosting, they are well camouflaged against the background of leaf litter or tree bark. Immatures are nearly identical, but have buffer feather edgings.

Common Poorwill
Phalaenoptilus nuttallii

L 7.5-8.5" | **WS** 17.5"

More often heard than seen, this is the smaller relative of the more conspicuous Common Nighthawk. Poorwills favor dry upland habitats east of the Cascades with rocky outcroppings and semi-open pine forest. They nest and roost on bare ground, favoring basalt rimrocks and dry forest floors, where their cryptic plumage keeps them well hidden. They are generally rare west of the Cascades, except for dry upslope areas in the southern Cascades and Siskiyou Mountains. Their tiny bill belies a massive mouth that allows them to capture insects on the wing. They are most active at dawn and dusk and may feed and call all night on calm, clear, moonlit nights. They get their name from their hollow whistled *poor will* song.

Adult. Much smaller and shorter-tailed, with shorter, more rounded wings, than the more frequently encountered Common Nighthawk. They lack the broad white wing patch shown by nighthawks.

Vaux's Swift

Chaetura vauxi

L 4.25" | **WS** 11"

Adult. Sometimes described as a "cigar with wings." Mostly dark charcoal-brown, with a paler tannish throat and rump.

Watching a vortex of thousands of birds funnel down into a chimney is clearly intoxicating, and the twilight gatherings of Vaux's Swifts have become spectator events in many Oregon towns. At the peak of fall migration in September, more than 2000 human onlookers attend the "swift nights" sponsored by the Audubon Society of Portland. Vaux's Swifts arrive in early April and are widespread breeders across most of Oregon, particularly in the more forested areas west of the Cascades. Except when they are sleeping and incubating eggs, they spend their lives on the wing. They build their nests inside hollow snags and brick chimneys. If you hear high-pitched twittering calls coming from your fireplace, you may have swifts.

White-throated Swift

Aeronautis saxatalis

L 6-7" | **WS** 13.25"

Adult. Distinctive white and black pattern, long narrow tail, and scimitar-like wings separate this species from other North American swifts.

These swifts are found almost exclusively around towering cliff faces and deep-cut basalt river canyons, where they perform remarkable high-speed aerial acrobatics. Smith Rocks State Park, the Crooked River Gorge, and the rimrock above Roaring Springs Ranch south of Frenchglen are among the most reliable places in Oregon to see this species. They are present from April through early September, and absent from the state during colder months. Call is a fast descending series of metallic or grating *jee, jee, jee, jee...* notes.

Black-chinned Hummingbird

Archilochus alexandri

L 3.75" | **WS** 4.5"

Black-chinned Hummingbirds are uncommon migrants and sparse breeders across much of eastern Oregon; they rarely stray west of the Cascades. They are generally uncommon from June to August in lowland valleys and stream corridors in the eastern half of the state. Spring and fall migrants frequent feeders in towns during May and then again in August, but typically become scarce or disappear altogether during the nesting season. When incubating and feeding young, nearly all hummingbirds feed more on insects and wild nectar, avoiding feeders.

Adult male. Uniform bronzy green head, back, and wings. Narrow gorget normally looks black, but a narrow band flashes brilliant iridescent violet in direct sunlight. Bill is longer than on most Oregon hummingbirds and is very slightly curved.

Adult female/immature. Bronzy greenish above and mostly whitish to dingy pale gray below. May show indistinct rows of small dusky-green feathers on the throat.

Anna's Hummingbird

Calypte anna

L 4" | **WS** 5"

This, the only hummingbird found year-round in Oregon, is the most frequently encountered hummingbird in western Oregon; it is also establishing new outposts east of the Cascades. Anna's Hummingbirds are resident in the Columbia Gorge east to The Dalles, and wintering Anna's are now regularly found in Bend. Remarkably, this species has been documented breeding in almost every month of the year. Young routinely appear in western Oregon as early as late February and early March. They are mostly low-elevation urban and suburban birds, depending on feeders from October to February. Males engage in courtship displays any time the sun is shining, even in the dead of winter. The "song" consists of a series of three burry, slurred notes as they ascend straight up before a steep J-shaped dive. At the bottom of the dive, they flare their tail to make a loud, sharp *chirp* as air rushes across the feathers.

Adult male. Mostly iridescent green to bronzy-green above, duller green to pale gray below. Long, flared gorget and crown feathers iridescent fuschia in bright sun. Lacks the clean white breast of other green-backed hummingbirds.

Adult female/immature. Iridescent green to bronzy-green above. Adult females generally show a small patch of ruby iridescence and green spotting on the throat, while immature birds are cleaner whitish on the throat and show less color on the flanks.

Rufous Hummingbird

Selasphorus rufus

L 4" | **WS** 4.5"

Harbingers of spring across much of Oregon, Rufous Hummingbirds are among our earliest neotropical migrants, showing up along the southern Oregon coast at the end of February and in the first days of March. A metallic wing buzz and *zee chuppity chup* calls announce the return of males, which arrive first and often dominate any feeder they frequent. They breed commonly along the outer coast, in the Coast Range, and along the western slopes of the Cascades. They are generally less common east of the Cascades. Adult males typically disappear by late July, with females and immatures lingering to about mid-September. They rarely overwinter in Oregon.

Adult male. Almost entirely rusty-orange above and below, with a narrow band of white across the breast. Bright iridescent orangish-red gorget may look green when not in direct sun. Green in plumage typically limited to the crown and wings, but some individuals show green on the back.

Adult female/immature. Mostly bronzy-green on crown back and rump, with extensive rusty wash along flanks and across the base of the tail. Throat mostly white with variable dark green spotting in the middle. Immature is less rusty on flanks, with cleaner whitish throat.

Calliope Hummingbird
Selasphorus calliope

L 3.5" | **WS** 4.5"

Oregon's smallest hummingbird is found primarily east of the Cascades, where it inhabits sub-alpine montane meadows and riparian stream corridors above 2,000 feet in elevation. A few strays are found west of the Cascades during spring migration. Calliopes are not as noisy as most hummingbirds, making only a soft bumblebee-like buzz with their wings when displaying and giving rapid chattering chips.

Male. Smaller than any other Oregon hummingbird, mostly green above and white below. Unique gorget, with fuchsia-colored feathers arranged in lines. Outermost gorget feathers longer and flared.

Female. Similar to female Rufous Hummingbird, but noticeably smaller, bronzy-green above and whitish below, with only a faint wash of rusty buff on flanks. Wings extend to or slightly past the tip of the very short tail.

Virginia Rail
Rallus limicola

L 9" | **WS** 13"

More often heard than seen, these secretive birds are are fairly
common breeders throughout the state, particularly at sites
with extensive freshwater marsh. Virginia Rails winter in the
western Oregon lowlands, and are quite numerous year-round
at sites such as Fern Ridge Reservoir near Eugene and Fernhill
Wetlands near Forest Grove. The easiest time to see this species
is July and August, when the juveniles are out exploring muddy
openings in the sedge and cattail marshes. Adults rarely linger
in the open before scurrying out of sight into the reeds. Their
most common calls are a series of *kidick, kidick, kidick* notes
and an explosive oinking *renka, renka, renka*. They can be
coaxed into vocalizing at any time of day or night by rapping
two stones together to mimic the *kidick* call.

Adult. Rusty brown and streaked above. Solid rusty on the breast, blackish belly with white
bars on sides. Face grayish. Long, slightly downcurved bill ranges from dull orangish to
bright red. Longish orangish legs and toes are chicken-like. Immatures (not shown) are dark
charcoal-colored version of the adult, with mostly dark bill. Newly hatched chicks look like
black cotton balls.

Sora

Porzana carolina

L 9" | **WS** 14"

Plumper and shorter-billed than most rails, this bird is more chicken- or quail-like in appearance. Like other rails, Soras are heard far more often than seen. Common to abundant breeders across the state, they nest in most freshwater marsh habitats, but prefer the shorter vegetation of wet meadows and seasonally flooded areas. Wintering occurs at some western Oregon sites, most notably Fernhill Wetlands near Forest Grove, where this species can be heard calling throughout the year. Call starts with a pair of upslurred whistles followed by a loud series of fast whinnying whistles, gradually descending and slowing.. Whinny call can be heard from considerable distance and may stimulate other rails to call. They also give a sharp *peek* or *weep* call.

Adult. Bright corn-yellow bill is short and sturdy. Mostly slaty gray below and a mix of brown and dusky-gray above with white streaks and spots. Face and throat are black. Greenish straw-colored legs and feet. Immature (not shown) generally like adult, but pale buffy below and more rusty brown above; bill smaller and dull straw-colored.

American Coot
Fulica americana

L 15" | **WS** 24"

Colloquially known as "mud hens," the superficially duck-like coot is in fact an aquatic rail. When feeding, coots tip up like dabbling ducks and even dive like diving ducks to reach underwater vegetation. They also graze on pondside lawns and forage on open mudflats. Out of the water, coots are long-legged with lobed toes. They are common nesters in low elevation wetlands and marshes throughout Oregon. They winter commonly along the coast and in the westside lowlands; they do not winter where the water regularly freezes, but are locally common from October to March at more temperate sites along the Columbia River and east of the Cascades. Although not often seen in flight, coots do migrate, sometimes gathering by the hundreds or thousands at favored staging areas. Vocalizations are an unmusical assortment of grating croaks, grunts and squawks.

Adult. Black head and neck, solid dark charcoal body, white undertail. White bill with partial dark band at tip. Blood-red eye. Juvenile (not shown) like adult in shape. Sooty brown body, whitish to gray foreneck and breast. Bill dark or horn-colored. Newly hatched chicks are black and fuzzy, with bare reddish skin on head.

Sandhill Crane

Antigone canadensis

L 47" | **WS** 78"

Sandhill Cranes are gregarious, forming large flocks both on the ground and in flight. Unlike Great Blue Herons, which are sometimes called "cranes," this species holds the neck and legs fully outstretched in the air. Stiff, shallow wingbeats. Famous for their dancing courtship displays, Sandhill Cranes are common breeders at Malheur National Wildlife Refuge and in marshy basins east of the Cascades. They also nest in wet meadows around larger lakes in the Cascades, but are rare west of the Cascades in summer. Winter viewing is best on Sauvie Island, just northwest of Portland, where more than a thousand cranes winter and thousands of spring migrants gather. Wintering is also common in the neighboring bottomlands on the Washington side of the Columbia . The loud, throaty calls of migrants can be heard from more than two miles away.

Adult. Nearly five feet tall, with long neck and legs. Gray, with white cheek and red crown. Long dark bill.

Immature. Fuzzy golden youngsters, referred to as "colts," look like gangly goslings as they tag along behind their parents.

Black-necked Stilt

Himantopus mexicanus

L 13.5–15.5" | **WS** 28"

No other North American bird has such long legs for its size as this aptly named species. Stilts arrive in early April, and are found both east and west of the Cascades through August. They are common breeders in the Klamath, Summer Lake, and Harney Basins and in many other eastern marshes. In recent decades, they have also colonized a number of wetlands in the Willamette Valley, including Fern Ridge W.M.A. and Baskett Slough N.W.R. They are fiercely territorial, greeting any and all intruders with a scolding series of loud *keep, keep, keep* calls.

Adult. Mostly jet black above and white below, with reddish-pink legs nearly twice the length of the body.

American Avocet

Recurvirostra americana

L 18" | **WS** 31"

This instantly recognizable bird is a common breeder around large marsh complexes and playa lakes in much of eastern Oregon. In recent years a pair or two have nested at Fern Ridge W.M.A., but they are otherwise rare west of the Cascades. The nests are usually located in plain view. In addition to loud calls, adults feign injury to draw predators away from their eggs and recently hatched young. Unlike most shorebirds, which probe and pick for food, avocets sweep their long upturned bills back and forth through the water to stir up prey. The most common call is a loud *kleek, kleek, kleek*.

Adult (breeding). Head and neck the color of a perfectly toasted marshmallow. Upperparts black and white, underparts white. Long black bill is distinctly upturned. Legs soft bluish gray.

Adult (non-breeding). Winter adults and immatures like breeding adult, but head and neck are pale pearl gray to whitish instead of orangish-brown.

Black Oystercatcher

Haematopus bachmani

L 16.5-18.5" | **WS** 28-36"

Oregon's heaviest shorebird has an exclusively coastal distribution. Oystercatchers can be found throughout the year around the bases of basalt sea stacks and along rocky shorelines. Outside the breeding season small flocks may be seen roosting together at high tide or coming to drink and bathe where small creeks empty into the ocean. They rarely spend time on open beach or mudflats. The loud call, a stuttering trill of whistled *wheep* notes, usually announces their arrival.

Adult. Large, plump shorebird. Body all-black to dark chocolate-brown. Long, sturdy bright red bill and bubblegum-pink legs. Conspicuous bright red ring around yellow eye.

Black-bellied Plover

Pluvialis squatarola

L 11" | **WS** 23"

This chunky Arctic-breeding shorebird is a habitat generalist, found on beaches, estuary mudflats, muddy lakeshores, flooded pastures, and even drier short-grass fields. Black-bellied Plovers are common to uncommon in winter along the coast and locally uncommon at a few favored Willamette Valley sites, with Fern Ridge W.M.A. the most reliable inland wintering location. East of the Cascades, they are rare to uncommon spring and fall migrants. They typically feed on estuary mudflats at low tide and move to open beaches and wet pastures at high tide. During the peak of spring migration from late April to mid-May, adults in stunning breeding plumage are a relatively common sight on open beaches, particularly Sunset Beach between Gearhart and the Columbia River mouth. Their loud whistled *pee-er-wee* can be heard from half a mile away.

Adult (breeding). Mostly jet black below, with gleaming white undertail. White forehead, crown, nape, and upper flanks. Back mottled white and black.

Winter adult/juvenile. Lightly mottled pale to medium gray above (juveniles warmer and browner), pale gray to whitish below. Conspicuous dark eye on plain gray to whitish face.

Snowy Plover
Charadrius nivosus

L 6-7" | **WS** 13.5"

Snowy Plovers nest in depressions in exposed coastal fore-dunes and playa lake margins in southeast Oregon. The tour loop at Summer Lake W.M.A. and Abert Lake are the best places to see inland-breeding plovers. Known nesting sites along the outer coast are generally closed to human entry, as disturbance leads to a high frequency of nest predation and abandonment. Beach closures and wire cages around nests have been successful, if sometimes controversial, in protecting coastal nesters. Modest numbers of Snowies winter along the Oregon coast in areas with light human traffic. Most coastal Snowy Plovers wear colored plastic leg bands to permit monitoring of this fragile population.

Adult (breeding). Small plover with short, sturdy black bill. Pale sandy upperparts, white below. Black markings on forecrown, behind the eye, and on the side of the neck.

Winter adult/immature. Same as breeding adult, but without black markings on head and neck. Sandy gray upperparts with smudgy spur on the side of upper breast.

Semipalmated Plover
Charadrius semipalmatus

L 7" | **WS** 14"

At first glance this bird looks like a miniature Killdeer with just one breast band. Though they don't breed in Oregon and rarely winter here, Semipalmated Plovers are common to uncommon spring and fall migrants across most of the state. They are most readily found on coastal beaches and estuary mudflats from mid-April to mid-May and then again from mid-July through September. They generally stay out of the water, preferring drier open beach and estuary margins. During fall migration they often visit drying reservoirs and lakebeds. Their loud, sweet *che wee* calls ring out over the calls of other shorebirds.

Breeding adult (Spring). Dirt-brown above, white below. Bill short and sturdy, with orangish base and black tip. Black band narrows at center of breast. Broad black band wraps across the forecrown and continues through the eye. White forehead.

Non-breeding adult/juvenile (Fall). Similar to breeding adult, but lacks black on head and breast. Breast band is brown like the back and wings and often incomplete across the breast.

Killdeer

Charadrius vociferus

L 10" | **WS** 19"

This noisy and ubiquitous bird is as likely to inhabit a playground, a gravel parking lot, or a muddy farm field as any more "typical" shorebird habitat. Killdeer have an odd relationship with humans, often building nests in places with heavy foot or vehicle traffic and then scolding us loudly when we get too close to their nests or young. These plovers lay eggs in a shallow, unlined depression in gravel or cobbles. They are famous for their "broken wing" displays, used by adults to draw predators away from nests and cottonball-sized fledglings. The loud two-note whistle *kill deer* is the source of their name. When agitated, they also give a piercing series of *dee, dee, dee* scold notes.

Adult. Plump, robin-sized shorebird, dirt-brown above and white below. Black and white face and breast, with two broad black breast bands and black and white face. Thick dark bill. Fledgling looks like a miniature fuzz-ball version of adult, but with a single breast band.

Whimbrel
Numenius phaeopus

L 17" | **WS** 32"

The smaller of Oregon's two curlew species is a common to
uncommon spring and fall migrant along the coast. Whimbrels
use their long, distinctly downcurved bill to probe for food in
mud and wet sand. They are most conspicuous during spring
migration from late April into early June, when scattered small
flocks are a common sight on coastal beaches and in larger
estuaries. They move into wet pastures to feed during high
tides, when flocks numbering into the hundreds gather in dairy
pastures east and south of Tillamook and southeast of Astoria.
Pasture lands between Port Orford and Bandon are the best
areas for seeing large numbers on the southern Oregon coast.
They are rare but annual migrants inland, usually appearing
singly. High fliers, Whimbrels are often heard before they
are seen. Call a loud accelerating trill of whistled *tew, tew
tew* notes.

Adult. All ages similar. Smaller, shorter-billed,
and more earth-brown than Long-billed
Curlew. Distinctive dark brown crown stripes.

Long-billed Curlew

Numenius americanus

L 19.5–25.5" | **WS** 10–12.5"

Oregon's longest-billed shorebird is common across much eastern Oregon in such short-grass lowland habitats as wheat stubble, alfalfa, and grassy breaks in the sagebrush steppe. Curlews arrive from their southerly wintering grounds in early April; they quickly start claiming nesting territories with aerial displays combining extended glides and bursts of fluttering wingbeats with mournful, drawn-out *cur-lee* calls. These inhabitants of dry grassland eat many grasshoppers, beetles, and other invertebrates. When disturbed, they give a fast stuttering series of *cu-leek* calls.

Adult. Crow-sized tawny bird with exceptionally long, downcurved bill. More warmly colored than the smaller Whimbrel and lacks dark crown stripes.

Adult flight. Bright cinnamon underwings in flight.

Marbled Godwit

Limosa fedoa

L 18" | **WS** 30"

Marbled Godwits are uncommon spring and fall migrants, mostly along the outer coast, but a few pass through the Klamath, Summer Lake, and Harney Basins in spring and fall. They occur regularly at many of the larger estuaries, including Youngs Bay, Tillamook Bay, Yaquina Bay, and Coos Bay. In spring migration they often feed on open beaches and, at high tide, in wet dairy pastures. Often found in large flocks of migrating Whimbrel. This species does not breed in Oregon, but individuals occasionally summer in the state. Godwits use the long bill to probe wet sandy beaches and estuary mudflats. Call is a series of loud *radica radica radica* phrases.

Adult. Very large sandpiper with long, pink-based blue-gray bill. Back spangled dark brown and buff; underparts warm cinnamon-buff, barred black in spring adults.

Flight. Warm cinnamon underwings and flight feathers are distinctive.

Ruddy Turnstone
Arenaria interpres

L 7" | **WS** 21"

This calico-patterned Arctic breeder is a scarce spring and fall migrant along the outer coast and a rare stray inland, most often found in large flocks of migrant shorebirds on open beaches. During April and May, Clatsop Beach between Gearhart and the Columbia River mouth is a reliable site. Unlike the Black Turnstone, Ruddy Turnstones are not as inclined to feed on rocky shores. A grating chatter is the most commonly heard vocalization in Oregon.

Breeding adult. Plump, thick-legged shorebird with distinctive calico pattern above. Head black and white. Back and wings black and rusty-brown. White below. Sturdy, slightly wedge-shaped black bill. Bright orange-red legs.

Juvenile. Immatures and non-breeding adults show muted head and breast pattern and more uniform brown back. Legs duller orangish straw color.

Black Turnstone

Arenaria melanocephala

L 8-10" | **WS** 17-18"

Black Turnstones don't nest in Oregon, but flocks of ten to thirty, often mixed with Surfbirds, can be found along the coast nearly year-round, dodging the splashing surf on rocks in the intertidal zone. Wintering flocks are often found on jetties; Barview Jetty at the mouth of Tillamook Bay and the South Jetty of Yaquina Bay are accessible sites for this species. Their dark plumage provides excellent camouflage against the blackish basalt, and they can go unnoticed until they flush with a grating chatter and unmistakable black and white wings. The sturdy bill is used to pry small invertebrates from rocks.

Adult. Plump, thick-legged, robin-sized bird. All ages and plumages similar. Nearly solid black on breast, head, back, and wings. White belly and undertail. Short, sturdy bill; dark legs.

Red Knot

Calidris canutus

L 10" | **WS** 23"

To know the Red Knot is to admire it. These long-distance migrants consume up to half their body weight during their long flights. Lying between two major migratory stop-overs—Grays Harbor in Washington and Humboldt Bay in California—Oregon is just a "whistle stop" for this intrepid sandpiper, which breeds in the Arctic and winters in Central and South America. It is rare to see more than a few a day along the Oregon coast, but driving the open beach between Gearhart and the Columbia River mouth in late April and early May or August and September offers the best chances to encounter this species. Call is a soft, double-noted *weet weet*.

Breeding adult. Plump, medium-sized sandpiper, rich cinnamon-reddish below, mottled black and pale gray above. Dark, strongly tapered medium-length bill. Legs black.

Non-breeding adult/juvenile. Nondescript gray above and slightly paler below; juvenile with neat, fine pale edges on wings. Weak whitish stripe above eye.

Surfbird

Aphriza virgata

L 9.5–10.5" | **WS** 17"

Almost never seen inland, this chunky, thick-billed sandpiper is found almost exclusively on rocky intertidal outcroppings and jetties, typically in the company of Black Turnstones; pure flocks of more than fifty birds are sometimes encountered. Aside from a few months in the Arctic to nest, Surfbirds reside in Oregon year-round. The call given by flushed birds is a soft, throaty chatter, but they are generally quiet away from the breeding grounds.

Breeding adult. Striking pattern of black, gray, and white mottling with bright rusty scapulars. Legs dull yellow. Bill mostly dark, with bright yellow base below.

Non-breeding adult. Uniform medium-gray head, breast, back, and wings. Bill duller than in breeding adult. White tail with black tip.

Sanderling
Calidris alba

L 8" | **WS** 15"

Sanderlings are the quintessential sandpipers seen in so many paintings and photographs of sandy beaches. Even non-birding beachgoers notice them. It's hard not to be fascinated by their ability to scurry back and forth, never seeming to misjudge the speed of the water washing onto the beach. During the height of spring and fall migrations, thousands mass on Oregon beaches such as the North Spit of Coos Bay and Clatsop Beach from Seaside to the mouth of the Columbia. Sanderlings are Arctic breeders, with the Pacific population wintering along the coast from British Columbia to southern Mexico. In recent decades, Oregon's wintering population seems to have declined. Call is a flat *wick*.

Adult. Looks mostly white September to May, with very pale gray back, white underparts, dark smudge at the shoulder. Black bill and legs. Breeding adult rusty brown on head, breast, and back.

Juvenile. Similar to winter adult, but heavily spangled black and buff above, with some buff wash on breast.

Dunlin
Calidris alpina

L 8" | **WS** 15"

This is western Oregon's most abundant wintering sandpiper and a common to uncommon spring and fall migrant state-wide as it travels to and from Arctic breeding groundsAlong the coast, Youngs Bay and Tillamook Bay typically host large wintering flocks. Thousands winter in the southern part of the Willamette Valley, where Fern Ridge Reservoir is a favored site, and t hey are also found in the vast rye fields and other short-grass and bare-ground habitats between Albany and Eugene. The sight of a large flock in distant flight can be especially impressive. Typical call is a trilled metallic *kree*.

Breeding adult. Bright rusty cap and back, mostly white below with dark streaks on breast and distinctive black belly patch. Fairly long black bill droops towards the tip. Black legs.

Non-breeding adult. Nondescript dusky gray-brown above and on breast; otherwise dingy white below.

Baird's Sandpiper

Calidris bairdii

L 7.5" | **WS** 15"

Typically moving through the Great Plains in spring and the interior west in autumn, the Baird's Sandpiper is an uncommon fall and rare spring migrant through Oregon. Most Baird's Sandpipers seen here are southbound juveniles, typically found from late July to September. They like open beaches and estuary edges, generally preferring drier and sandier substrates. Inland, they are often found around the margins of drying reservoirs, particularly in eastern Oregon. Their abundance varies from year to year: flocks of more than a hundred have been found at eastside sites such as Thief Valley Reservoir in Union County and Antelope Reservoir in Malheur County, but are usually found mixed with migrant flocks of Western Sandpipers. A dry, rough *brrrrt* is the common call note.

Juvenile. Warm buffy brown above and on breast, with scaly-looking back and wings. Featureless face makes the eye look large. Long-winged and short-legged, with a rangy look. Black bill and legs. Spring adult similar, but spangled rather than scaled above.

Least Sandpiper

Calidris minutilla

L 6"   **WS** 11"

North America's smallest sandpiper is a common spring and
fall migrant statewide and an uncommon wintering bird west
of the Cascades. Leasts don't breed in Oregon, but can be found
in the state almost any day the year at almost any place with
water and some mud, from the smallest farm puddle to the
largest estuary. Unlike most other sandpipers, they tend stay
out of the water, preferring rank muddy spots with interspersed
vegetation. During migration, they often appear in mixed
flocks with Western Sandpipers. Call is a high-pitched,
burry *brrreeet*.

Breeding adult. Sparrow-sized
sandpiper. Mostly dark brown
to reddish brown above and
on breast. White below. Legs
straw-yellow. Bill mostly dark,
short, and slightly drooped.

Non-breeding adult. Dark
brownish gray to gray
above and on breast. White
belly and undertail. Legs
greenish-yellow.

Pectoral Sandpiper
Calidris melanotos

L 9" | **WS** 18"

These mid-sized sandpipers, somewhat resembling an over-sized Least Sandpiper, are long-distance migrants that breed in the Arctic and winter in South America. In Oregon, Pectorals are uncommon fall and rare spring migrants; most birds seen in the state are southbound juveniles between August an mid-October. Pectoral Sandpipers like the muddy margins of ponds, drying reservoirs, seasonal puddles, coastal estuaries, and wet recently-plowed fields, but tend to avoid open beaches and sandier habitats. Year-to-year abundance fluctuates wildly. Call is grating, throaty *churrr*.

Juvenile. Similar to adult, but rustier above, with warm reddish-brown cap and more obvious supercilium. Base of bill yellowish brown.

Breeding adult. Earth-brown above, with pale-edged back and wings. Darker brown cap, pale supercilium. Heavily streaked breast abruptly separated from white belly. Legs straw yellow. Bill mostly black, slightly drooped.

Western Sandpiper

Calidris mauri

L 5.5-7" | **WS** 10-14.5"

Western Sandpipers neither nest nor winter in Oregon, but for a few weeks each spring and fall they are the most numerous shorebird in the state. Upwards of 50,000 a day have been seen flying past coastal headlands during spring migration, and it's common to find thousands in many estuaries and along outer beaches from mid-April to mid-May. They are common to uncommon migrants inland. The mostly coastal fall migration of adults starts by the first of July; by mid-August the adults are gone, replaced by the flight of juveniles, which migrate later than their parents. Very small numbers occasionally winter, but Western Sandpipers are generally absent from Oregon from mid-October through early April. Typical call is a burry, high-pitched *jeet*.

Breeding adult. Rusty cap, ear coverts, scapulars, and upper back. Upperparts otherwise streaky gray. Underparts white with dense dark chevrons across breast and sparse chevrons on flanks. Bill and legs black. Bill slightly drooped at tip and variable in length.

Juvenile. Gray-brown cap and back. Underparts mostly unmarked, with slight buffy wash and sparse streaking on sides of upper breast.

Short-billed Dowitcher

Limnodromus griseus

L 11" | **WS** 19"

Less common and widespread than the very similar Long-billed Dowitcher, Short-billed Dowitchers are mostly found along the coast in Oregon. The movement of northbound adults is compressed, generally occurring during the last week of April and the first two weeks of May. Southbound adults, which breed in the Arctic, move through Oregon during July and are rarely seen in the state after the first week of August. Juveniles appear along the coast by early August and are typically gone from Oregon by mid-September. Fall migration is the best time to find Short-billeds inland; most are juveniles. They are extremely rare in winter. The distinctive call of the Short-billed is a hollow, throaty *tu tu tu*.

Breeding adult. Warm cinnamon-buff on underparts limited to breast and upper belly. Strong dark barring on mid-flanks. Dingy white to buffy lower belly and undertail. Long, thick-based tubular bill straw-greenish at base, darker towards slightly drooped tip. Legs straw-greenish. Juveniles similar.

Long-billed Dowitcher
Limnodromus scolopaceus

L 11" | **WS** 19"

Nesting far to the north of Oregon, this is the expected dowitcher in the state most of the year, particularly away from the outer coast. Thousands gather at Malheur N.W.R. and Summer Lake W.M.A. from late July well into October. West of the Cascades, Fern Ridge W.M.A. is among the best places to see this species, especially between August and October, when hundreds are usually present. They winter uncommonly west of the Cascades. Long-billed Dowitchers are habitat generalists: any wet spot with mud will do, but they prefer freshwater, and are often more numerous inland than along the coast. Apparent bill length is not useful in dowitcher identification. The distinctive call of the Long-billed is a sharp, hi-pitched *keek*, typically repeated in two- to five-note bursts.

Breeding adult. Almost completely cinnamon-brown below. Sparse dark barring on flanks. Long tubular bill, slightly thinner at base and straighter at tip than in Short-billed. Legs straw-greenish.

Non-breeding adult. Uniformly medium-gray above and on breast, dingy white below. Juveniles similar.

Wilson's Snipe

Gallinago delicata

L 10" | **WS** 18"

These marsh denizens spend most of their time hidden in dense vegetation, or sitting motionless and well camouflaged along the edges of seasonal ponds and flooded pastures. During the breeding season, snipe become extroverts, perching on roadside fenceposts and claiming their territory for all to see. . Seemingly every third fencepost has a calling snipe on it during May and June. Malheur N.W.R. and the seasonally flooded pastures around Burns and Hines are the best places to see this bird up close. The territorial call is a repetitive *jicka, jicka, jicka* that accelerates into a louder *jick, jick, jick* at the end. The flight display is accompanied by an otherworldly *hu, hu, hu, hu, hu* that rises in pitch, produced by air rushing across the tail feathers as unseen snipe descend from high overhead.

Adult. Plump. Heavily patterned with black, brown, white, and buffy stripes and barring. Long, straight, dark straw-colored bill. Striped head pattern unique among Oregon shorebirds. Legs straw-colored. All ages similar in appearance.

Spotted Sandpiper

Actitis macularius

L 8 " | **WS** 15 "

Spotted Sandpipers are loners compared to most sandpipers. It unusual to see more than four or five loosely grouped together even in migration. They breed commonly all across Oregon, but are scarce wintering birds in the state. They prefer sites with narrow rocky or muddy shoreline and exposed logs with nearby grassy edges. Sewage treatment ponds are one of their favored nesting habitats and generally reliable for seeing them in migration. They also nest around small wooded ponds and lakes at all elevations, even high in the mountains. Their movements and flight style are distinctive. Feeding birds constantly rock, bobbing their tails up and down. In flight, the wingbeats are shallow and fluttering with breaks of gliding. Common flight call is a sharply whistled *weet-weet*, frequently heard overhead at night from migrants.

Breeding adult. Crown, nape, back, and wings olive-brown with some dark spotting and barring. Underparts white with blackish spots. Whitish supercilium and dark line through eye. Legs fleshy yellow. Short, straight bill mostly yellow-orange with dark tip.

Non-breeding adult/immature. Dark brownish-gray above. Clean white below, with spur of brownish gray at shoulder. Less obvious whitish supercilium and dark eyeline. Bill darker than adult's.

Solitary Sandpiper

Tringa solitaria

L 9" | **WS** 16"

As the name implies, this is not a bird prone to flocking.
Finding even two Solitary Sandpipers together is unusual away
from breeding grounds. This species has summered and perhaps
nested at two high lakes in the Cascades, but is otherwise an
uncommon spring and fall migrant through Oregon. Solitaries
are most often found around seasonal puddles, stock ponds,
and small wooded ponds with muddy channels bordered by
vegetation. It is rare to find one in more open habitat. Call is a
piercing, whistled *weet weet*, higher pitched than the similar
call of the more common Spotted Sandpiper.

Adult. Suggests small dark yellowlegs. Dark dusky-brown upperparts with neat white
spotting. White underparts. Dark vest on upper breast. Distinctive black and white
barring on sides of tail. Conspicuous white eye ring. Dark medium-length bill. Legs
greenish straw color. Juvenile similar, with buffy spotting above.

Lesser Yellowlegs

Tringa flavipes

L 10" | **WS** 24"

Virtually identical in all plumages to the larger and heavier-billed Greater Yellowlegs, Lessers are the less expected yellowlegs in Oregon. They are uncommon to scarce spring and fall migrants, with most sightings of southbound juveniles in August and September. They are rare in winter. Lesser Yellowlegs are graceful, moving with more measured and even steps than the awkward manner of the Greater. When seen, side by side, the size and structural differences between the two species are obvious, but some smaller and shorter-billed male Greaters may be mistaken for this species. Call is a combination of much softer single and doubled *tu* notes; does not give the loud three-note call that identifies the Greater.

Juvenile. Smaller and shorter-billed than nearly identical Greater Yellowlegs. Earth-brown above with fine whitish spotting. Underparts mostly white, with fine gray streaking on breast. Thin bill is slightly longer than the head length. Orange-yellow legs.

Greater Yellowlegs
Tringa melanoleuca

L 12" | **WS** 24–28"

The Greater Yellowlegs does not nest in Oregon, but this large, boisterous, gangly shorebird is common to uncommon statewide during spring and fall migrations, and winters uncommonly west of the Cascades. Greater Yellowlegs are habitat generalists, occurring almost anywhere there is a sizable puddle, including seasonally flooded pastures and more permanent wetlands and estuaries. The herky-jerky feeding motions are a helpful identification clue. They don't form large flocks, but can be found in scattered groups of thirty or more. The loud three-note *tew, tew, tew* calls are easily heard from up to a quarter of a mile away.

Breeding adult. Heavily spangled black, white, and gray upperparts. Underparts heavily streaked and barred. White eye ring. Bright orange-yellow legs.

Juvenile. Dark earth-brown above with fine whitish spotting. Underparts mostly white, breast with fine light gray streaking. Long dark bill is about twice as long as the head. Legs orange-yellow. Winter adults similar, but plain gray and unspotted above.

Willet

Tringa semipalmata

L 15" | **WS** 26"

This large, stocky shorebird, which suggests an oversized yellowlegs, breeds commonly in Oregon's Great Basin marshes, but barely remains to winter in the state. Malheur N.W.R. is the best place to see this species in Oregon. Willets are ubiquitous on the pastures and wetlands flooded by the spring and summer runoff from Steens Mountain. A small flock winters on Coos Bay, but they are rare anywhere else in western Oregon. Willets are rather nondescript except in flight and in their territorial display, when the distinctive black and white under-wing pattern and rollicking *pill-will-willet* song make them unmistakable.

Non-breeding adult. Cold medium-gray above. Pale gray to whitish below. Grayish olive legs. Bluish-gray bill with dark tip.

Breeding adult. Mostly gray, with black and white spangling on upperparts and variable brown barring below. Legs grayish olive. Long, sturdy bill mostly dark with horn-colored base.

Wandering Tattler

Tringa incana

L 10–12" | **WS** 19.5–21.5"

The best way to see this bird is to hang out on coastal jetties during spring and fall migration. Tattlers tend to feed down in the splash zone on jetties and rocky outcrops, where their mostly gray plumage makes them hard to spot against the gray rocks. Learning the distinctive loud call will help in finding them. The typical vocalization, given mostly by birds in flight, is a loud series of sharply whistled *kree* notes that often accelerate into a hollow, whistled trill.

Breeding adult. Uniformly medium-gray above, with pale grayish-white supercilium. Underparts heavily barred gray. Yellow legs. Medium-length sturdy bill.

Non-breeding adult. Solid gray above and on breast. Belly and undertail dingy white.

Wilson's Phalarope

Phalaropus tricolor

L 9 | **WS** 15-17"

The late summer gathering of this species at Abert Lake may well be the most impressive of Oregon's many avian spectacles. Hundreds of thousands descend on this playa lake to feed on brine flies, stirring them up by spinning in place on the water, before the long flight to their wintering grounds. Wilson's Phalaropes nest commonly in the marshy basins of southeastern Oregon, arriving in late April and typically leaving by early October. In recent decades they have also established a handful of breeding outposts in the Willamette Valley. The larger and more colorful female selects mate, lays eggs, then moves on to mate with other males, leaving incubation and chick-rearing to her original mate. Unlike its two smaller relatives, the Wilsons' Phalarope does not migrate over the open ocean. Vocalizations, often given in a series, include a muted nasal honk, given by both sexes, and a hollow, low-pitched *wonk*, given only by females.

Adult female. Larger and longer-billed than male. Bluish-gray cap, nape, and back. Rich chestnut on sides of neck and wing coverts. White below. Rusty wash on forecrown. Legs black. Needle-like black bill. Adult male (not shown). Overall muted in color and pattern. Browner back and paler chestnut on neck, noticeably shorter black bill than in female.

Red-necked Phalarope

Phalaropus lobatus

L 7.5 | **WS** 15"

Don't be fooled by the outwardly fragile appearance of the
Red-necked Phalarope. This bird is remarkably hardy, spending
most of its life offshore as it travels between Arctic breeding
grounds and wintering areas in tropical oceans. In Oregon,
migrant flocks are often seen passing coastal headlands and
farther offshore during pelagic trips.. It's certainly a surprise
to see small shorebirds landing on the water between ocean
swells and then spinning in their trademark way to stir up
prey. They are sometimes found mixed in with other shorebirds
on open beaches, and modest numbers of Red-neckeds pass
through the interior, where they are most often found on sewage
ponds and other permanent impoundments. Call is a flat,
high-pitched *kip* or *clip*.

Juvenile. White face and underparts, black cap and smudge through eye. Heavily
streaked black, white, and buff back. After early September, back is mostly pale gray with
black scapulars. Female larger and more colorful than male (not shown). Mostly dark
slaty gray above with buffy stripes on back and rich reddish brown on neck. Throat and
belly white. Needle-like bill.

Red Phalarope

Phalaropus fulicarius

L 8.5 | **WS** 17"

This is the most sea-going of the phalaropes and the most robust. Though Red Phalaropes are abundant spring and fall migrants, the migration occurs well offshore. When major weather systems roll in off the Pacific between November and January, storm-battered waifs are sometimes deposited all over the landscape, even many miles inland. During these *wrecks* one is likely to see a Red Phalarope just about anywhere there is a puddle, from roadside ditches to the parking lot at the grocery store. When conditions are more benign, though, it is generally necessary to go well offshore on a boat to see this species up close. Call is a sharp *pik*.

Adult female. Rich cinnamon-brown neck and underparts. White cheek, black cap and face. Back streaked black and white. Bill mostly yellow, sturdier than other phalaropes. Adult male similar, but not as richly colored.

Winter adult/juvenile. Pale gray above with limited dark streaking. Underparts and head white. Black smudge through eye, less dark on crown than Red-necked. Dark bill is thicker than in other phalaropes, flesh-colored or yellow at base.

Bonaparte's Gull

Chroicocephalus philadelphia

L 13" | **WS** 31"

Bonaparte's Gulls seen in Oregon usually do not sport the black head, which is seen only on adults from May to July. They are uncommon to common spring and fall migrants statewide and occasionally overwinter, but they do not nest here. Northbound movements peak in early or mid-May, when it is possible to see hundreds moving just offshore or stopping to rest and feed on open beaches and estuaries. Fall migration is more protracted, running from mid-September into early November. Upper Klamath Lake is among the most reliable places to see this species east of the Cascades, with September and October assemblages there sometimes numbering into the thousands.

Breeding adult. Very small gull with black head and thin black bill. Entirely white below, pale gray above. In flight, wing shows broad white leading edge. Blood-red legs and feet.

Non-breeding/ immature. White head with distinctive dark gray or black spot behind eye. Adults plain gray above. Immatures have broad blackish bar across folded wing and pink legs and feet.

Franklin's Gull

Leucophaeus pipixcan

L 13-14 | **WS** 33-37"

The Franklin's Gull summers commonly in southeastern Oregon, but is rarely found on coastal beaches, or west of the Cascades at all. These long-distance migrants arrive in mid-April from their southern hemisphere wintering grounds. The only black-headed gull that breeds in the state, several thousand pairs nest at Malheur N.W.R. Smaller numbers nest in the neighboring playa basins in the southeastern quadrant of the Oregon; the breeding range has expanded in recent years. Once nesting is completed, the southbound migration begins, and they are generally gone from the state by September. They often fly high, catching insects on the wing. The loud, nasal *meow* call is distinctive as it rings out over the sagebrush.

Breeding adult. Larger and darker gray above than Bonaparte's Gull. Black head, with dark blood-red bill. Broad white broken eye ring. In flight, band of white separates black wingtip from rest of gray upperwing. Legs dark reddish-brown.

Non-breeding/immature. Similar to breeding adult, with partial hood. White around base of bill, on forehead and chin.

Heermann's Gull

Larus heermanni

L 18-21 | **WS** 41-45"

Heermann's Gulls are unconventional in many ways, starting with their ash-gray plumage, which is unlike any other North American gull. They breed off western Mexico, then disperse north between July and October into cooler, food-rich waters. They often follow Brown Pelicans, which have a similar nesting range and post-breeding dispersal. When pelicans return to the surface after a plunge dive, a bevy of opportunistic Heermann's Gulls is usually there to gather up the scraps. Call is a nasal and somewhat duck-like *ow*.

Summer adult. Almost entirely dark ashy gray, slightly darker above than below. Head white. Bright red bill with a black tip. Legs black. By September, head fades to pale gray.

Immature. Plain sooty gray or sooty chocolate-brown. Bill fleshy pink to reddish with dark tip.

Mew Gull

Larus canus

L 16–18 | **WS** 42–45"

Small and delicate, the Mew Gull is often described as pigeon-like in appearance. Head bobs as it walks about feeding. This Arctic breeder starts appearing along the coast in mid-September, and is abundant there from November the birds migrate north again in April. Thousands inhabit sodden dairy pastures from late fall to early spring, pulling up worms and other invertebrates. Upwards of 20,000 have been counted in the sprawling pastures around Tillamook during midwinter. More modest numbers winter in the Willamette Valley, but when strong winter storms pound western Oregon, Mews move to more sheltered inland valleys by the thousands, retreating to the coast only when the weather improves. They also feed on estuary mudflats or just offshore, especially as pastures dry out. Call is a sharp, squeaky *mew*, shorter than most other gulls' calls.

Adult (above). Small, slender gull. Medium-gray above, white below. Rounded pigeon-like white head, mottled with brown except during nesting season. Small, thin, unmarked yellow bill. Legs short and straw-yellow. Comparatively long, black-tipped wings. Immature (right). Gray mantle. Off-white head, wings, and underparts smudged and mottled grayish brown. Dark wingtips. Slender pink-based bill with dark outer half.

Ring-billed Gull

Larus delawarensis

L 18" | **WS** 44"

This aptly named gull is widespread in Oregon year-round.
Ring-billed Gulls breed only east of the Cascades, mostly
on islands in the Columbia River and in the marshes around
playa lakes in southeastern Oregon. They feed on drier fields,
pastures, and open spaces, including parking lots, that most
other gulls avoid. They are the most abundant wintering gull in
the southern Willamette Valley, where they feed by the hundreds
on the grass seed fields of Lane and Linn Counties. They are
surprisingly sparse on the outer coast. Modest numbers use
coastal estuaries, but they do not join other gulls in offshore
feeding flocks and aren't often found on the open beach. Call a
rising two-note squeal.

Adult. Mid-sized gull. Distinctive black band on yellow bill. Back and wings pale gray.
Wingtips evenly black above and below. Pale yellowish eye. Legs yellow. Immature (inset).
Wing coverts spangled brown and white. Head and underparts white with limited fine
brown to blackish mottling. Bill yellowish-pink at base with black tip. Legs fleshy pink.

Herring Gull
Larus argentatus

L 25" | **WS** 56"

Herring Gulls represent a minority of the large gulls that winter in Oregon, where they are outnumbered by Glaucous-winged and Western Gulls. They do not breed in the state, and are scarce at any season east of the Cascades. They are uncommon along the coast, in the Willamette Valley, and along the lower Columbia River from September to April. Like other gull species, Herrings may move inland during strong winter storms. More prone to scavenging than other gulls, they are often seen around landfills. A lone gull seen feeding on a sheep carcass in the southern Willamette Valley is almost always a Herring Gull. Call is a prolonged and mournful *meeyew*.

Immature. Finely streaked pale head with contrasting heavily mottled body. Bill mostly pinkish with dark tip.

Winter Adult. White head with dusky streaking and mottling. Mantle paler then other large gulls. Jet-black wingtips. Bill pale yellow with red spot. Eye pale yellow to whitish. Legs and feet pink.

Western Gull

Larus occidentalis

L 22–26" | **WS** 47–57"

This large, bulky, dark-backed species is Oregon's default "seagull," abundant year-round all along the coast. Western Gulls breed on all of the state's major sea stacks and on many larger offshore rocks. The only breeding gulls at most coastal sites, they can be readily found on open beaches, offshore rocks, in estuaries and boat basins, and around rocky creek mouths the empty directly into the ocean. A few wander inland to the Willamette Valley during winter, but they are almost strictly a coastal species.

Western Adult. Only Oregon gull with un-mottled white head year around. Dark gray back and wings. Jet-black wingtips. In flight, underside of flight feathers slaty. Eye dark. Bill bright orangish-yellow with red spot near tip. Legs and feet pink. Some paler individuals are probably hybrids with the more northerly Glaucous-winged Gull.

Adult flight. Dark gray above with black outer flight feathers.

Immature. Heavily mottled brown body. Bill black. Legs and feet pink.

California Gull

Larus californicus

L 18.5-21.5" | **WS** 51"

This wide-ranging gull can use almost any habitat. California Gulls generally breed away from saltwater, but spend most of the year near it. Breeding occurs in the marshes in the Great Basin and on islands along the Columbia River. Once fledged and independent, juveniles flood to the outer coast during August and September. The Columbia River is a major migration corridor for westbound juveniles starting at the end of July. Many juveniles hatched to our south disperse north as well, resulting in gatherings of tens of thousands on Oregon's beaches and estuaries. As winter approaches, most California Gulls move south out of the state, but they can be found along the coast any month of the year.

Breeding adult. Clean white head, medium-gray mantle and wings. White below. Black wing tips. Legs yellow. Yellow bill with red and variable black spots.

Non-breeding adult. Similar to breeding adult. Heavy mottling on head and nape creates a hooded appearance. Dull yellow bill with red and black spots on mandible.

Immature. Chocolate-brown to cinnamon-brown, with spangled coverts, scaly mottled pattern overall. All-dark bill in July and early August turns pink with a dark-tip by early September. Older immatures with black-tipped blue-gray bill and blue-gray legs.

Glaucous-winged Gull

Larus glaucescens

L 19.75-23.25 | **WS** 47-56"

This, the default "ballfield" and park gull in the Willamette
Valley in winter, is also abundant along the outer coast, feeding
by the hundreds in wet dairy pastures. Glaucous- Glaucou-
winged Gulls breed from the mouth of the Columbia River
north to Alaska. Non-breeders routinely summer in Oregon.
Call is a loud piercing *keow*, typically repeated several times.

Adult. Head heavily blotched gray most of the year, clean white only during spring and
summer. Gray on primary tips same shade as mantle and wing. Thick bill is pale yellow
with red spot; darkens to orange-yellow in nesting season. Eye dark. Legs and feet pink.
Some darker individuals are probably hybrids with the more southerly Western Gull.

Adult flight. Gray wings with white trailing edge. Eye dark. Legs and feet pink.

Immature. Highly variable, pale sandy-brown to darker brownish gray. Subdued pattern in wing coverts. Wingtips same color as wing. Legs and feet dull pink. Bill thick and all dark.

"Thayer's" Iceland Gull

Larus glaucoides thayeri

L 20-24 | **WS** 45-54"

These northerly nesters arrive late in fall, usually not until October, and are mostly gone from the state by mid-April. They occur almost exclusively along the coast and in the Willamette Valley, and are rare east of the Cascades away from the Columbia River. They tend to be pasture feeders along the coast, and use wet grassy fields and athletic fields inland, often mixing with larger, paler-winged Glaucous-winged Gulls. Calls include a high-pitched *kee-ya* and longer shrill *meeyew*.

Winter Adult. Smaller, more delicate, shorter-legged, and rounder-headed than other large gulls. Dusky head markings blotchy rather than crisp. Pale yellow bill with red spot is shorter and narrower than Herring Gull's. Eye usually dark.

Immature. Medium sandy brown with intricately patterned mantle and wing. Primaries medium- to dark dusky brown with paler edges. Bill all black until late winter, then shows some flesh color at base.

Caspian Tern

Hydroprogne caspia

L 20" | **WS** 45"

Caspian Tern is the largest and one of the most widespread terns in the world. Caspians have traditionally nested at Malheur N.W.R. and other playa lake basins in southeastern Oregon; today, thousands inhabit Youngs Bay during the nesting season, and there are huge colonies on the lower Columbia River . Efforts using artificial nesting islands to lure terns to new sites away from the Colubmia's salmon have mostly failed. Spring arrival is in mid-March, and most depart by late September. From late June on, the calls of adults and juveniles ring out over breeding colonies and coastal estuaries. Young remain dependent on adults for food for several months. Juvenile begging call is a wheezy, high-pitched, up-slurred whistle. Adult call is a loud, scratchy *krowk*.

Adult. Massive bright red bill. Cap generally remains solid black from March to September. In flight, wingtips are solid black above and below. Legs and feet black. Juvenile (not shown) with orangish bill with dark tip. Cap solid blackish. Highly patterned mantle and wing. Leg color varies from brownish orange to near black.

Black Tern

Childonias niger

L 10" | **WS** 24"

Black Terns' feeding habits suggest an oversized swallow. They do take small fish and tadpoles, but much of their diet consists of insects gracefully plucked off the surface of the water. They frequently swoop and change direction and often pause to hover as they fly along searching for food. Black Terns are common to abundant breeders at larger marsh complexes in Harney, Lake, and Klamath Counties, and are uncommon breeders at many smaller marshes east of the Cascades. In recent decades they have colonized several sites in the Willamette Valley, notably Fern Ridge W.M.A. west of Eugene. Immature and winter adult plumages are suggestive of a very small gull. Call is a series of raspy, chattering *keeks*.

Juvenile. Mostly white head and underparts. Partial black hood surrounds eye and wraps over crown. Mantle, wings, and tail medium- to dark gray. Brown on upperparts fades quickly. Legs and feet flesh-colored.

Breeding adult. Almost entirely black head and body. Silvery gray wings and square tail. Lower belly and undertail white. Bill long, thin, and all black. Legs and feet black.

Common Tern

Sterna hirundo

L 14"   **WS** 30"

The Common Tern, one of the more uncommon tern species in Oregon, is a regular spring and fall migrant through the state. On rare occasions coastal flights number into the hundreds, but most sightings involve twenty or fewer birds. Inland, they are usually far from shore over larger lakes and reservoirs. If there is a reliable site for this uncommon and unpredictable species, it is Fern Ridge Reservoir in Lane County, where Common Terns are seen most years in the latter half of May and the first two weeks of September. Calls include a nasal *kip* and grating *kee-er*.

Breeding adult. Mostly pale gray body. Pale gray upperwing darkens to black in outer primaries. Smudge of black on the underside of outermost primaries. Bill dark red with black tip. Legs and feet red.

Non-breeding adult/ Immature. Diagnostic dark bar on shoulder. Partial black cap extends from the eye across nape. Forehead white. Bill black in non-breeding adults, dark reddish with dark tip in immatures.

Forster's Tern

Sterna forsteri

L 13" | **WS** 31"

Superficially similar to several other tern species, the Forster's Tern is a common nester in freshwater marshes, rarely found within 100 miles of the Pacific in Oregon. It arrives in mid- to late April and generally migrates out of the state by late September. Forster's Terns are found at wetlands all across eastern Oregon and at some of the marshier lakes in the Cascades. They also summer along the Columbia River from the Deschutes River mouth east. They are particularly abundant breeders in the Klamath, Lake, Harney, and Umatilla County wetlands. Rare strays west of the Cascades, they have nested at least once at Fern Ridge Reservoir in Lane County. Call is a raspy downslurred *kerr*.

Adult breeding. Long-tailed, white-bodied tern with heavy, orange-based bill. Upperparts pale gray, shading to silvery white at wing tips.

Adult non-breeding. Satiny black cap replaced by elongated black mask surrounding eye. Nape is white or diffusely streaked, never solid black. Bill black, feet duller than breeding orange.

Elegant Tern

Thalasseus elegans

L 15.5-16.5" | **WS** 42"

Like Heermann's Gulls and Brown Pelicans, Elegant Terns are Mexican breeders that disperse north after nesting in search of food. In most years, Oregon sees a few hundred individuals between July and October; few go farther north than Curry and Coos Counties. More than four hundred may gather around the Columbia River mouth in good years, but the highest counts typically come from the mouth of the Rogue River at Gold Beach, where twice that many have been recorded. Call is a loud, grating *keer-ick*, easily heard a quarter mile away.

Non-breeding/immature. Slender, medium-sized tern with long, thin, pumpkin-orange bill. Extensively white forehead. Black crest extends from eye across the nape. Long, narrow wings are pale gray above.

Red-throated Loon

Gavia stellata

L 25" | **WS** 43"

Though this smallest of the loons breeds only far to the north of our state, Red-throated Loons are common to uncommon along the Oregon coast between October and early May, and are occasionally found inland, mostly along the Columbia River. During peak migration in April and May and again in September and October, hundreds and sometimes thousands a day can be seen passing near shore off coastal headlands. Boiler Bay State Wayside in Lincoln County is a good site to witness these flights. When feeding in estuaries or on the ocean, Red-throated Loons tend to prefer shallower water, sometimes diving for prey in water no more than a foot deep. They habitually hold their bills pointed slightly upwards. Like all loons, the legs and feet extend past the tail in flight, and the long narrow wings appear to be centered on the body as the birds fly low over the water.

Breeding adult. Rich brownish red patch on throat. Head medium-gray with fine streaking on crown and nape. Dark back without distinct markings. Red eye. Thin black bill.

Non-breeding adult/immature. Extensive white on face and neck extends above eye. White on flanks above water line. Dark gray back with fine white speckling. Thin grayish bill.

Pacific Loon

Gavia pacifica

L 23-29" | **WS** 43.5-50.5"

At the height of fall migration in October, the massive flights of Pacific Loons passing the Oregon coast can be mind-numbing. During peak morning pulses, hundreds of birds per minute fly by low over the water, and on the best days, flocks stream past all day. It has been estimated that as many as 100,000 migrant Pacific Loons have flown by Boiler Bay State Wayside on a single day. Spring numbers are smaller, but the migration is still quite impressive, especially as most birds are in their dapper breeding plumage. This species spends most of its time in saltwater and is the least likely of Oregon's three regularly occurring loons to venture inland. Nevertheless, strays to the interior appear annually in October and November, typically on large lakes and reservoirs, particularly in the Cascades.

Breeding adult. Stunning pattern of black, white, and gray. Throat black. Head medium-gray, transitioning to pale silvery gray on hind crown and nape. Black back with bold white barring. Medium-sized black bill.

Non-breeding adult/ immature. Dusky gray above, white lower face and breast. No white showing above waterline on flanks. Eye mostly surrounded by gray feathering. Narrow chin strap across white throat on adults. Bill grayish.

Common Loon

Gavia immer

L 32" | **WS** 46"

Although Common Loons don't nest in Oregon, their iconic yodeling can occasionally be heard during spring as adults begin courtship rituals before heading north to breed. This largest and most widespread of the state's three regularly occurring loons can found here most of the year, particularly along the coast. The expected species in Oregon's coastal estuaries, Common Loons also winter and stop in migration at many of the larger lakes and reservoirs across the state. Non-breeders occasionally summer along the coast and on lakes high in the Cascades. Wickiup Reservoir in Deschutes County is a favored stopover for fall migrants, with annual high counts in the low hundreds. Coastal migratory flights are not as spectacular as those of Pacific and Red-throated Loons. Migrants typically fly high above the horizon.

Breeding adult. Head and neck bands look black, but are iridescent green in good light. Blackish back densely spotted with white. Heavy dagger-like black bill. Blood-red eye.

Non-breeding adult/ immature. Dark gray above and white below. No white showing on flanks above waterline. Eye mostly surrounded by gray feathering. Peaked forecrown and blocky head shape. Heavy silvery-gray bill can appear whitish in bright sun.

Black-footed Albatross

Phoebastria nigripes

L 43" | **WS** 80"

Albatrosses, massive birds with seven-foot-plus wingspans, spend most of their lives at sea and in flight. Rarely seen from land, the Black-footed Albatross is virtually guaranteed if you have the stomach to take a pelagic (deep-oecan) trip in Oregon waters. Seeing an albatross is always a thrill, well worth the potential discomfort. Black-footed albatrosses are most numerous from April to October, but are present offshore year-round. At their peak in August and September, hundreds can be tallied on a single trip. Exceptionally efficient fliers, albatrosses use wind shear off long ocean swells and dynamic soaring to fly remarkable distances with only occasional wing flaps.

All ages. All ages similar. Almost entirely dark sooty brown, slightly paler and grayer below. Varying amounts of white on face. Older adult paler-headed. Dull grayish pink bill with dark gray tip and base.

Sooty Shearwater

Ardenna grisea

L 17" | **WS** 41"

Shearwaters fly low over the water, alternating rapid flurries of shallow wingbeats with long, flat-arcing glides, taking advantage of wind shear off of waves to fly great distances very efficiently. Digital tracking has revealed that Sooty Shearwaters fly upwards of 40,000 miles annually between the South Pacific breeding grounds and "wintering" waters in the North Pacific. Unlike most tubenoses, Sooty Shearwaters are routinely visible from land. Feeding flocks and passing migrants often pass within a quarter mile of shore. Peak abundance in Oregon waters occurs in August and September. The area just south of the Columbia River mouth is a favored gathering site, the best place in Oregon to see assemblages of tens or even hundreds of thousands. Boiler Bay State Wayside and similar coastal headlands are dependable for more modest numbers from May to October. Feeding birds dive from a sitting position on the water, using their wings for propulsion.

All ages. All ages similar. Uniformly dark sooty brown, looks black at a distance. In flight, note silvery gray underwing flash. Slender dark bill with tube on top.

Pink-footed Shearwater

Puffinus creatopus

L 18" | **WS** 43"

Oregon's largest and second most abundant shearwater is less likely to be seen from land than the Sooty, but is equally expected on pelagic trips. Breeding in the South Pacific and "wintering" north of the Equator, Pink-footed Shearwaters are most abundant off Oregon from August to October. They are most likely to be seen from shore in late September and early October, particularly after strong westerly winds. Lower-lying headlands such as Boiler Bay State Wayside in Lincoln County offer the best viewing angle for spotting shearwaters from shore. Compared to Sooty Shearwater, this species' flight style is lazier and more deliberate, with less rapid wingbeats.

All ages. All ages similar. Dark gray-brown head and upperparts. White below with dark undertail. Underwings mostly white, with extensive dark on trailing edge and dark smudging on "armpits." Dull pink bill with dark tip. Legs and feet dull pink.

Fork-tailed Storm-Petrel

Oceanodroma furcata

L 8" | **WS** "

Storm-petrels are amazingly hardy robin-sized seabirds that come to land only to breed. Fork-tailed Storm-Petrels nest in burrows on offshore rocks, coming and going at night. Only a few pairs nest in Oregon. This species is seen on most Oregon pelagic trips, sometimes by the hundreds, and it is the storm-petrel most likely to be seen from land. Fork-taileds driven ashore by strong westerly winds sometimes linger for days feeding around bay mouths. In most years, a few are seen in the jetty channel of Yaquina Bay in Lincoln County, usually between October and March. Inland records are truly exceptional. Fork-tailed Storm-Petrels feed like swallows, fluttering and gliding low over ocean swells, then plucking prey from the surface while in flight or briefly sitting on the water. Their flight style is steadier and more direct than that of other storm-petrels.

All Ages. All ages similar. Almost entirely pale ashy gray. Darker smudge through eye. "V" pattern on upper parts. Black bill is short, sturdy, and tubed.

Leach's Storm-Petrel

Oceanodroma leucorhoa

L 8" | **WS** 19"

Despite being the most numerous breeding storm-petrel on Oregon's offshore rocks, sightings of Leach's Storm-Petrels are remarkably few, even on pelagic trips. They spend their lives far out to sea beyond the continental shelf, coming and going from nesting burrows only at night. Repositioning cruise ships, which usually travel more than fifty miles offshore, offer the best opportunities to see this species and other deep-water seabirds. After strong westerly winds, storm-driven waifs of this species have reached the Willamette Valley several times, including one that spent the day flying up and down the downtown Portland waterfront. Flight style is buoyant and somewhat erratic; feeding birds sometimes patter on the water.

All ages. All ages similar. Uniformly dark sooty brown, usually looks black. Rump white. Ashy gray wing coverts create pale bars on long, bent wings. Short, black tubed bill.

Brandt's Cormorant

Phalacrocorax penicillatus

L 27-31 | **WS** 42"

Strictly a coastal bird, the Brandt's Cormorant is the least
abundant of Oregon's three cormorant species. Despite
spending most of their life within a mile of shore, Brandt's
Cormorants rarely venture away from saltwater or come farther
inland than estuary entrances, where they can be seen roosting
on rocks, pilings, and bridge abutments. Common breeders on
many of the state's sea stacks, many pairs nest right below the
lighthouse at Yaquina Head in Lincoln County, the best place to
see this bird up close during the breeding season. Cormorants
dive for food, living mostly on fish. Grunting vocalizations are
mostly heard on breeding grounds.

Breeding adult. All-dark plumage with glossy sheen. Sky-blue throat pouch bordered by tan feathering. White plumes on face and back. Stubby legs with large webbed feet. Bill long and narrow, with slightly hooked tip.

Non-breeding flight. All-dark plumage. Tan throat patch. Holds neck fully extended in flight; head is slightly bulbous and thicker than neck.

Pelagic Cormorant

Phalacrocorax pelagicus

L 20-30" | **WS** 39-47"

Oregon's smallest cormorant is abundant along the coast throughout the year, breeding on offshore rocks and bay-mouth bridge abutments and pilings. Although the name "pelagic" ("deep-ocean") suggests otherwise, this species spends its life within a mile of shore, and is a common sight flying in and out of estuaries. Rare inland, but strays have been found up the Columbia River to at least Portland. Dives for fish. Rarely vocalizes away from nesting grounds.

Breeding adult. All-dark plumage with glossy green sheen. Facial skin deep red. Large white flank patches. Long, thin dark bill with slight hook at tip. Non-Breeding (not shown). Barely visible patch of red facial skin. Flies with pencil-like neck and slender head fully extended.

Double-crested Cormorant

Phalacrocorax auritus

L 27.5–35.5" | **WS** 45–49"

Larger and bulkier than its two coastal relatives, the Double-crested Cormorant is the default species inland, breeding statewide pretty much anywhere there is a large body of water with fish in it. It is resident around most lakes, reservoirs, and large rivers that don't routinely freeze in winter, and occasionally visits smaller ponds and sewage treatment ponds to feed. This species' numbers declined precipitously during the DDT era, but have recovered dramatically since that insecticide was banned in 1972. Double-crested Cormorants now appear to be more numerous than ever all across North America. The world's largest nesting colony, near the Columbia River mouth, has even become a conservation concern: tens of thousands of cormorants now live in this area, feasting on salmon smolt as they make their way to the ocean.

Breeding adult. All-dark plumage with bronzy gloss. Bright yellow-orange throat patch. Bushy crests with white plumes behind emerald-green eyes. Long bill, usually held pointed slightly upwards, has a hooked tip. Non-breeding adult/immature flight (inset). Paler and browner than other cormorants. Tan to whitish on breast. Yellow throat patch and facial skin. Neck held crooked during flight, creating the illusion of flying "uphill."

American White Pelican

Pelecanus erythrohynchos

L 50-65" | **WS** 96-114"

The distribution of Oregon's freshwater pelican has changed significantly in the last generation, particularly west of the Cascades, where it was once rare. American White Pelicans traditionally nested on islands in the Columbia River east of The Dalles, Upper Klamath Lake, and in the Warner Valley. Nesting resumed at Malheur N.W.R. in the 1990s after a half century without breeding pelicans, and the first westside nesting colony was established along the lower Columbia River in 2010. Non-breeders and post-breeding dispersants now frequent many sites in the Willamette Valley. Sauvie Island near Portland and Fern Ridge W.M.A in Lane County typically have sizable flocks from July to September. A few now winter along the Columbia River and in the Willamette Valley. They eat predominantly fish, often working cooperatively to herd fish into the shallows. American White Pelicans are high fliers, flocks using thermal uplift and circling like raptors as they gain altitude.

All ages. Unmistakeable massive white bird with black trailing edge to wing. Huge bill with yellow-orange pouch.

Brown Pelican
Pelicanus occidentalis

L 39–54″ | **WS** 79″

Given its size and odd appearance, the Brown Pelican is astoundingly adept as it dives for food or gracefully glides along low over the water. This species is a conservation success story: pollution by pesticides and other chemicals caused widespread nesting failure, and in 1970 the Brown Pelican was federally listed as endangered. After DDT was banned in 1972, Brown Pelicans steadily increased in the Pacific Basin, and they are once again abundant July to October visitors along Oregon's shores. These saltwater birds breed off the Baja peninsula, then disperse north to cooler, food-rich waters after nesting. In Oregon, they can be seen roosting on jetties and nearshore rocks, and on docks and pilings inside coastal bays. They rarely stray inland.

Breeding adult. Body and wings mostly chocolate brown. Buffy golden forehead and face with white hind crown and nape. Reddish throat pouch.

Immature. Uniformly brown, with pinkish-brown throat pouch.

American Bittern

Botaurus lentiginosus

L 28" | **WS** 36–42"

This big brown heron is better known for its sound than its appearance. The unmistakable gulping *oonk-a-loonk*, mostly heard during the breeding season, may be the only indication that this stealthy bird is present in a wetland. American Bitterns creep along marsh edges with painfully deliberate steps as they feed. If startled, they freeze with neck extended and bill pointed upward, using their striped plumage as reed-like camouflage. Bitterns nest in freshwater marshes statewide, but are most abundant in expansive wetland complexes like those at Malheur N.W.R., Upper Klamath Lake, and Fern Ridge W.M.A. They winter sparingly in Oregon, and are hard to detect when they aren't vocalizing.

All Ages. All ages similar. Upper parts a mix of reddish browns and buffy streaks. Throat and breast striped reddish brown and whitish. Bill medium-length, sturdy and straw-colored. Yellow eye. Greenish yellow legs and feet.

Great Blue Heron

Ardea herodias

L 38–54" | **WS** 66–79"

North American's largest heron, with its with long legs and neck and upright posture is often mistakenly called a "crane." Common year-round in Oregon, Great Blue Herons are colonial tree-nesters, forming large rookeries, usually in cottonwood forests, along major rivers and around coastal bays, large lakes, and reservoirs. The large stick nests are easily seen before the trees leaf out. Great Blues start courting and occupying nest sites by early March, and by June the incessant *tik, tik, tik* calls of recently hatched chicks fill the air around rookeries. Much of their winter feeding is in pastures and open fields away from water, with voles and field mice making up a big part of their diet. The most commonly heard vocalization from adults is a loud croaking squawk when they are flushed.

Adult. Tall, with upright posture and long legs and neck. Plumage mostly bluish gray. Black shoulder and brown patch at bend of wing. Mostly white head with black crown stripe. Long, dagger-like orangish yellow bill. Yellow eye. Flight. Unlike cranes, holds neck pulled back when flying.

Great Egret
Ardea alba

L 39" | **WS** 54"

The stately and graceful Great Egret is Oregon's largest white heron, roughly twice the size of the far less common Snowy Egret. Over the past half century this species has greatly expanded its range in the state, particularly west of the Cascades, where it is generally the only egret. Like its relative the Great Blue Heron, the Great Egret is a habitat generalist found along rivers, bays, lakes, and ponds and in flooded pastures; during the winter months, it too goes "mousing" in drier pastures and fields. It is a colonial tree-nester, sometimes forming mixed rookeries with Great Blues. Formerly bred only in southeastern Oregon, but in recent decades egrets have established several nesting colonies west of the Cascades. Rarely vocalizes, but guttural grunting calls sometimes heard as they flush.

All ages. All ages similar. Large, totally white heron. Long black legs. Long, dagger-like orange-yellow bill.

Snowy Egret

Egretta thula

L 24" | **WS** 36–39"

This small, delicate white egret with the "golden slippers" was once prized for its exquisite plumes, which were used to adorn women's hats in the nineteenth and early twentieth centuries. Eventually, laws were passed to end the slaughter of this and other plumed species. The Snowy Egret is an uncommon nester in the marshes of southeastern Oregon and a rare stray west of the Cascades. Malheur N.W.R. offers the best opportunity to see this bird. Aside from a few birds near Empire on Coos Bay, Snowy Egrets are generally absent from the state during the winter months.

Adult. Small white heron. Long, thin black bill surrounded by yellow facial skin. Legs black. Toes bright yellow.

Green Heron

Butorides virescens

L 18" | **WS** 26"

Oregon's smallest heron is uncommon and reclusive at all seasons. Found mostly west of the Cascades, it is locally rare to uncommon in lowlands east of the Cascades. Green Herons frequent small ponds, wooded sloughs, and wooded wetlands. They tend to perch on low branches and brush that overhang water, waiting for unsuspecting prey to swim by. Pairs nest singly, not in colonies like other herons. Nests are typically well hidden in cedars or other dense conifers. Common flight and alarm call is a loud, raspy *skew*.

Adult. Crow-sized heron. Dusky green above, sides of neck and breast rich chestnut. Throat and center of breast striped chestnut-brown and whitish. Dark dagger-like bill. Straw-yellow legs.

Black-crowned Night-Heron

Nycticorax nycticorax

L 25" | **WS** 44"

This stocky, neckless, nocturnal heron is typically seen sleeping. Night-herons roost during the day in dense brush and small trees along waterways, rarely more than twenty feet off the ground. They can be hard to spot as they stand motionless deep in the branches. They are common breeders in the Klamath, Summer Lake, and Harney Basin marshes, and locally uncommon nesters elsewhere east of the Cascades. Breeding has never been confirmed west of the Cascades, but has been suspected around Fern Ridge Reservoir and other Willamette Valley sites, where juveniles turn up annually in mid-summer. A good place to see this bird is along the Link Canal in downtown Klamath Falls. Outside the breeding season, dozens roost in the trees near the Lake Ewauna end of the canal.

Adult. Black crown and dusky-green back, otherwise medium-gray. Thick, black, dagger-like bill. Yellow legs and red eye. Immature. Mostly earth-brown. Heavily streaked underparts and head. Whitish and buffy spotting on back and wing. Large yellow eye. Bill yellowish below, dark above. Legs greenish.

White-faced Ibis
Plegadis falcinellus

L 18-22" | **WS** 32-36"

Breeding numbers of Oregon's only regularly occurring ibis species have mushroomed over the last forty years. While only about 200 pairs bred in the state in the 1970s, today thousands of pairs nest in the Harney Basin, where they arrive mid-April. This remains the best place to see White-faced Ibis, but they breed in nearly all of the playa lake basins across south-central and south-eastern Oregon, and regularly stray to the westside. Small flocks appear annually in the Willamette Valley and occasionally on the outer coast, usually between late April and early June. White-faced Ibis feed in seasonally flooded pastures and grassy wetlands. They often form mixed colonies with other herons and egrets. Nests are built over water in bulrushes and cattails, as protection from terrestrial predators. Most vocalizing is soft nasal grunting.

Breeding adult. Plumage is highly iridescent chestnut-brown and green. Red facial skin surrounded by white. Legs pinkish red, darker at the joint. Long, downcurved bill is dark horn.

Non-breeding adult/immature. Plumage less iridescent. Head and neck paler, finely streaked. No white around dull pinkish-brown face. Dark eye and legs.

Turkey Vulture
Cathartes aura

L 25-32" | **WS** 67"

Guided by an incredible sense of smell, Turkey Vultures are uncanny in their ability to locate decaying flesh. With no talons or bill capable of dispatching live prey, their diet consists entirely of carrion. Lightweight, hollow wing bones allow them to soar almost constantly with infrequent wing flaps, using thermal uplift to gain altitude. The shallow "V" of the wings and rocking motion in flight are helpful in separating Turkey Vultures from other large soaring raptors. Vultures are found statewide in Oregon, arriving in late February and lingering into October. A few overwinter annually in the southern Willamette Valley and occasionally along the south coast and in the Umpqua and Rogue Valleys. Nests are hidden in small caves, hollow logs, slash piles, and other dark recesses. Adults are usually silent.

Flight. Under side of flight feathers are silvery gray and semi-translucent, contrasting with darker underwing linings. Appears almost headless.

Adult perched. Larger and longer-winged than Red-tailed Hawk. Extremely dark brown plumage usually looks black. Tiny red head is mostly unfeathered. Small pale yellow tip on bill. Pinkish legs and feet.

Osprey
Pandion haliaetus

L 23" | **WS** 63"

This black and white fish-eating raptor, found around the
world, is between eagles and the Red-tailed Hawk in size.
Ospreys arrive in Oregon in early March and leave by October,
nesting commonly anywhere with a sizable body of water.
Ospreys were heavily affected by DDT, but the population
seems to have recovered and may even be larger than ever.
Flood control reservoirs and other impoundments have been
a boon to this species, which eats only fish. Ospreys plunge
talons-first into the water, often completely submerging before
coming up with a fish. In flight, they hold their wings bent
at the wrist, a distinctive posture not seen in other raptors.
Ospreys typically raise two or three chicks in large platform
nests made of sticks. Utility poles, pilings, snags, and dead-
topped trees are common nest sites. Call is a loud piercing
whistle that can be heard from at least a quarter mile away.

All ages. All ages similar. Head and underparts white,
with blackish mask through eye. Upper parts dark
chocolate-brown, often look black. Black and white
underwing with large dark patch at the wrist. Thick
legs and large feet pale gray.

White-tailed Kite

Elanus leucurus

L 12.5–15" | **WS** 42"

Stunningly beautiful and graceful, White-tailed Kites are locally uncommon residents of coastal pastures and the Rogue, Umpqua, and southern Willamette Valleys. These mid-sized hawks often hover as they search for prey in deep grass, then set their wings in a steep "V" before dropping straight down to capture voles and field mice. Their breeding status in Oregon is poorly understood, as they seem to disappear during the nesting season. In winter, kites roost in deep grass, often communally with Northern Harriers and Short-eared Owls. Well-known roosts at the end of Royal Avenue at Fern Ridge W.M.A. and along Diamond Hill Road west of I-5 in Linn County are great sites to watch these species gather in the evening. Call is a quiet yelping whistle.

Adult. Head, tail, and underparts white. Blackish eye smudge. Back and wings light gray, with distinctive black shoulder patches. Immatures show some brown on head and mantle.

Northern Harrier

Circus hudsonius

L 18-19.5" | **WS** 40-46.5"

The conspicuous white patch at the base of tail and owl-like face make this low-flying open-country raptor readily identifiable in all plumages. Unlike most birds of prey, Northern Harriers have easily distinguished male and female plumages. Resident statewide, harriers can be seen hunting over almost any type of treeless landscape. Small rodents are their typical prey. They nest and roost on the ground; in the winter months, they roost communally in deep grass with Short-eared Owls and, in some places, White-tailed Kites. Flight style includes much gliding and banking with wings held in a shallow "V." Typical call is a soft, thin whistle.

Adult male. Gray head and upperparts. Whitish below. Long tail with white patch at base. Black wingtips.

Adult female/immature. Earth-brown and mottled above. Buffy underparts streaked brown. Immatures have cinnamon underparts. White base to tail.

Sharp-shinned Hawk

Accipiter striatus

L 11"　|　**WS** 21"

Oregon's smallest hawk is uncommon statewide from September to March and a locally uncommon to rare nester in the state's heavily forested mountain ranges. Like the other short-winged, long-tailed birds in the genus Accipiter, Sharp-shinneds hunt smaller birds in dense woodlands and other tight spaces; they are not open-country hunters. During the winter they take advantage of bird feeders for an easy meal. Most Sharp-shinneds nest north of Oregon and winter to our south, but migrants are the most abundant fall raptor at the Bonney Butte in Hood River County, the state's only Hawkwatch International monitoring station. Barely jay-sized, males are considerably smaller than females. Flight style is a mix of rapid wingbeats and short glides. Insistent and piercing *keek, keek, keek* calls normally heard only on breeding grounds.

Juvenile flight. Dark earth-brown above. Pale underparts with heavy streaking from breast to undertail. Head barely protrudes from forward-pressed wings. Square-cornered tail.

Adult. Dark bluish gray crown, nape, back, and wings. Dense rusty barring below. Broad light and dark gray bars on square-cornered tail.

Cooper's Hawk
Accipiter cooperii

L 16" | **WS** 28"

Probably Oregon's most urban diurnal bird of prey, Cooper's Hawks are increasingly common nesters in wooded neighborhoods and routine visitors at backyard feeding stations; they are certainly the state's most common Accipiter year-round. Roughly crow-sized, they are larger than the similar Sharp-shinned Hawk, though in this species, too, males are smaller than females. Cooper's Hawsk are more inclined than Sharp-shinned to hunt in open and semi-open country. During courtship, adult Cooper's Hawks fly high in wide circles with exaggeratedly slow, deep wingbeats and white feathers fluffed out around the base of the tail. Nests are generally well hidden high in dense trees. The high-pitched *kee-eer* call of begging calls of juveniles are the best indication of a nearby nest. Adults give a series of loud, sharp *kek* notes.

Juvenile flight. Upperparts dark earth-brown. Streaking below is heaviest on breast, sparser and finer on belly and undertail. Leading edge of the wing is straight, with head projecting noticeably in front of the wing. Tail corners rounded. Adult. Dark charcoal-gray cap and dark bluish-gray upper parts separated by paler gray nape. Dense rust-colored barring below. Broad light and dark gray bars on tail. Tail corners rounded.

Northern Goshawk

Accipiter gentilis

L 21-25 | **WS** 41-46"

The largest and least abundant Accipiter is an uncommon breeder in all of Oregon's major mountain ranges except the Coast Range, where it is at best rare. Secretive and hard to find, Northern Goshawks inhabit dense montane forests from about 2,000 feet to near timberline, normally building their nests high in the canopy They are easiest to locate when loudly begging young are in the nest or just fledged. Nearly the size of Red-tailed Hawks, goshawks are aggressive defenders of young and nest sites, and will take a swipe at humans with razor-sharp talons if approached too close. They may venture out into more open country during winter, but remain hard to detect at any season. Begging call is insistent and protracted *keeah, keeah, keeah*. Adult call is a slightly softer, less urgent *weeah, weeah, weeah*.

Juvenile. Heavily mottled dark brown upperparts. Underparts evenly and heavily streaked with dark brown from throat to undertail. Rounded tail corners. Yellow eye.

Adult. Dark gray cap, nape, and upperparts. Pale gray with dense dark gray barring below. Conspicuous whitish line above red eye.

Red-shouldered Hawk

Buteo lineatus

L 20" | **WS** 40"

The richly colored Red-shouldered Hawks of the west coast are among North America's most eye-catching raptors. They started expanding into Oregon about four decades ago, first appearing in Curry County, and are now uncommon residents across most western Oregon lowlands and locally quite common on the south coast. They are also regularly found east of the Cascades, particularly around Bend and Klamath Falls, and in the Harney Basin. In flight, the rapid shallow wingbeats and long tail can cause juveniles to be misidentified as Northern Goshawks. They often perch upright, looking straight down, on fenceposts and utility wires. Preferred habitat is semi-wooded riparian areas, pasture edges, and broken woodland. Diet includes small rodents and snakes. Territorial call is a loud, insistent *keeah, keeah, keeah.*

Adult (above). Rich cinnamon head and underparts, solid on breast but barred on belly and undertail. Back brown with whitish bars. Black and white mottled wings, black tail with narrow white bars. Juvenile (left). Smaller than Red-tailed Hawk. Dark brown head and upperparts. Heavy pale mottling on wings. Underparts pale, with heavy dark streaking on breast changing to bars on the belly and lower flanks.

Rough-legged Hawk

Buteo lagopus

L 19 | **WS** 49"

This tundra nester winters in Oregon, arriving in October and departing by April. Rough-legged Hawks are more often seen sitting on the ground than in trees. When they do perch, it is usually closer to the ground than Red-tailed Hawks, often in short trees along field edges. Hunting Rough-legged Hawsk frequently hover. Adult males and females are distinct in plumage, unlike other species of Buteo. Most of Oregon's wintering birds are juveniles and adult females, which are similar in appearance. The whitish heads and extensively light tails might suggest a small Bald Eagle at first glance. They depend on expansive grassy areas for hunting, and thus are more abundant east of the Cascades and where rye and other short grasses are grown in the southern Willamette Valley. West of the Cascades, conversion of grassland to orchards, nurseries, vineyards, and berry patches has greatly reduced the habitat for this species.

Light morph adult (female). Creamy white head and breast. Dark brown back and upperwing. Broad dark band across belly. Underwing creamy white with large dark patches at wrist. Creamy white tail with broad dark band. Small bill.

Dark morph adult. Almost entirely dark brown to blackish above and below. Tail mostly whitish with dark band. In flight, dark wing linings contrast with white undersides of flight feathers.

Swainson's Hawk

Buteo swainsoni

L 19–22" | **WS** 47–54"

This long-distance migrant winters as far south as
Argentina, returning to Oregon to nest in early April and
departing by early October. Swainson's Hawks are open-
country birds, preferring the vast agriculture fields, grasslands,
and sagebrush steppe east of the Cascades; they rarely stray to
western Oregon. When hay and alfalfa fields are mown, Swainson's Hawks gather in numbers to feast on the bounty of insects
and rodents. They are particularly abundant on irrigated fields
in Harney, Lake, Klamath, and southern Deschutes Counties
and the dryland wheat fields of Sherman, Gilliam, Morrow, and
Umatilla Counties. Highly variable in appearance, with light
and dark morphs, and birds with intermediate plumages. Long
wings often held up in a slight "V." Wingtips tapered and more
pointed than those of other hawks in the genus *Buteo*.

Light morph Adult. Solid sooty brown
head and back and breast, with little or
no mottling. Face grayer, with white
around base of bill and on throat. Belly
and undertail area off-white with modest
barring. Tail minimally patterned. In
flight, underwing linings clean white.

Dark Morph Adult. Almost entirely dark
chocolate-brown above and below, with
modest paler barring on lower belly.
Yellow cere over nostrils. Yellow legs. In
flight, wing linings are paler and more
mottled than the flight feathers.

Red-tailed Hawk

Buteo jamaicensis

L 19" | **WS** 49"

North America's most widespread and abundant soaring hawk is the default Buteo across Oregon at any season. When a large hawk is seen, a good rule of thumb is that it's a Red-tailed Hawk until proven otherwise. This species is highly variable, with light, dark, and intermediate birds. It is a habitat generalist, but is normally found hunting small mammals in open and semi-open landscapes. Red-tailed Hawks typically perch on exposed tree branches and utility poles. They build stick nests in the canopy of woodland edges, and courting pairs can often be seen circling high over the nest. The call, a protracted screeching *keee-errrrr*, is used universally in commercials and movies whenever any species of raptor is shown.

Light morph adult. Dark earth-brown head and back with light spotting on shoulders. Mostly whitish below, with a variable band of streaks across belly. Brick-red tail with narrow dark band and paler tip.

Dark morph adult. Typically all dark chocolate-brown with brick-red tail. In flight, solid dark wing lining contrasts with whitish undersides of flight feathers.

Juvenile flight. Similar to light-morph adult but without red in tail. Broader band of streaking on belly. Dark bar on leading edge of underwing just inside the wrist is diagnostic for this species.

Ferruginous Hawk

Buteo regalis

L 22-27 | **WS** 52-56"

The large, pale Ferruginous Hawk is the southerly equivalent of Rough-legged Hawk. It, too, is an open-country bird, found almost exclusively east of the Cascades in areas where trees are sparse. Ferruginous Hawks are uncommon nesters across the southern tier of counties in southeastern Oregon and locally common where alfalfa is raised. They should be looked for on fields around the tiny hamlets of Hampton and Riley on Highway 20 between Bend and Burns; they are also reliably found around Crane and Princeton east of Malheur N.W.R and in the Fort Rock and Christmas Valley area of northern Lake County. Most Ferruginous Hawks leave for the winter, but one or two winter each year in the Rogue Valley, the only place west of the Cascades where they are expected at any season. Dark-morph birds are generally rare in Oregon.

Light morph adult. Larger and paler overall than any other large Oregon raptor. Pale rusty back and upperwing. Mostly white from below, with rust-colored thighs. Tail mostly white, rusty towards the tip.

Golden Eagle

Aguila chrysaetos

L 30" | **WS** 70-80"

All-dark Golden Eagles are generally devoid of field marks, and might be passed off as a Turkey Vulture or smaller dark-morph hawk from a distance. They are birds of arid canyonlands, sagebrush steppe, and basalt rimrock, feeding mostly on jackrabbits, ground-squirrels, and occasionally carrion. They are most common in the drier southeastern quadrant of Oregon, where they are resident. Nests, usually built on rimrock outcroppings, are used for decades. Soaring birds hold the wings in a shallow "V." Golden Eagles appear much smaller-headed than a Bald Eagle, creating a more vulture-like profile in flight. Full adult plumage is attained in four or five years.

Adult. Uniformly dark chocolate-brown with golden-tipped feathers on nape and neck.

Sub-adult/juveniles. Immature birds have white at the base of the tail and white patches in the outer wing. May or may not show golden nape.

Bald Eagle

Haliaeetus leucocephalus

L 33" | **WS** 80"

Bald Eagles are a common sight in Oregon skies and no longer listed as endangered. They nest most commonly on the coast, along major rivers, and around large lakes and reservoirs, and are less common breeders in the arid southeastern corner of Oregon. Pairs return to use the same massive stick nest each year. A must-see spectacle is the annual gathering of Bald Eagles in the Klamath Basin, where Lower Klamath N.W.R. hosts an incredible density of wintering eagles. The largest roost in the Lower 48, at Bear Valley west of the refuge, contains hundreds of eagles from October to March. Call is a series of downslurred piping whistles.

First-year immature. Mostly dark chocolate-brown. White mottling on underparts, underwing, and base of tail.

Adult. Unmistakable large soaring bird with white head and tail. Large yellow bill.

Barn Owl

Tyto alba

L 12.5–15.75" | **WS** 39.5–49"

As its name implies, this species commonly roosts and nests in barns. Barn Owls can be found in nooks and crannies high in the rafters, sleeping by day and wreaking havoc on local rodent populations by night. They also nest in rimrock cavities, artificial nest boxes, and even gaps in stacks of baled hay. Most numerous around farms, pastures, and open fields, they can occasionally also be heard giving their loud hissing *schhhick* calls as they fly over urban and suburban neighborhoods. Their diet, mostly rats and mice, allows them to be habitat general-ists. It is estimated that an adult Barn Owl kills 1,500 rats annually. With a little practice, humans can imitate the call, which often results in an owl coming to investigate the source.

All ages. All ages similar once fully feathered. Buffy golden-brown and gray above, white below. Face pattern suggestive of an apple sliced in half.

Flammulated Owl

Psiloscops flammeolus

L 6-7" | **WS** 16"

Most birders go a lifetime without ever seeing or even hearing a Flammulated, but field studies show that this owl is a far more abundant breeder in Oregon than many observers think. This highly migratory, soft-spoken tiny owl nests in old woodpecker holes deep in mid-elevation montane pine forests, far from human populations. Flammulated Owls arrive on the breeding grounds in May, after wintering mostly south of the U.S.. They are presumably gone from Oregon by October. Day-roosting Flammulated Owls are sometimes found during migration, typically in isolated patches of trees such as those at Malheur N.W.R. headquarters. They feed predominantly on insects, including many moths. Soft, deep single *hoop* sometimes preceded by a quick and even quieter double-noted introduction, *hoo-hoo HOOP.* Calling Flammulateds are often much closer than they sound.

All ages. All ages similar. Very small owl without feathered "ear" tufts. Cryptic mottled gray plumage with buffy brown face, rich buff scapulars, and large dark eyes.

Western Screech-Owl
Megascops kennicotti

L 7.5-10" | **WS** 21.5-24.5"

Oregon's smallest owl with "ear" tufts, the Western Screech-Owl can often be found close to home, even in semi-urban and suburban areas, where it responds readily to whistled imitations of its bouncing-ball series of hollow whistles. Screech-owls inhabit residential yards, small parks, modest woodlands, and streamside riparian corridors that are too small to support larger owls like Barred and Great Horned. They roost and nest in tree cavities, often with their faces visible at the cavity opening during daylight. Although they are found statewide, numbers are greatest west of the Cascades. Diverse diet includes small rodents, amphibians and even beetles. Occasionally heard during the day.

All ages. All ages similar. Appearance suggests that of a miniature Great Horned Owl. Plumage cryptic, mottled gray and brown with blackish bars and streaks. Large yellow eyes. Conspicuous "ear" tufts.

Great Horned Owl

Bubo virginianus

L 22" | **WS** 48"

Large, loud, and prone to perching in plain view, this is among the most easily seen of Oregon's owls. Classic "hoot owls," Great Horned Owls are common statewide residents, dominating the night skies in any habitat they choose. They usually nest in old hawk nests in trees, but also use barns and rimrock openings. Nesting starts early, with western Oregon pairs on eggs by late February. Great Horneds are known to kill other birds of prey, including smaller owls and hawks. They become active at dusk, when they can be seen perched on tall conifers, utility poles, and wires before flying off to hunt. Song is a stuttering series of five or six deep hoots.

Adult. Large, bulky owl with distinctive "ear" tufts ("horns"). Large yellow eyes. Cryptic, mottled gray-brown plumage. Warm buffy-brown face. Dense black barring below.

Snowy Owl
Bubo scandiacus

L 20-28 | **WS** 50-57"

Large all-white owls need no introduction. Snowy Owls are irregular winter visitors from the Arctic, no more than one or two appearing in Oregon most years and absent altogether in others. Every eight or ten years, however, major flight brings dozens to coastal dunes, most consistently around the south jetty of the Columbia River. They also occur with some regularity on the open grasslands of Morrow and Umatillla Counties and around airports and other wide-open spaces in the Willamette Valley. They are even occasionally found roosting on suburban rooftops in suburban neighborhoods. They rarely vocalize away from the breeding grounds.

All ages similar. Large all-white owl with variable black barring. Immatures and females more heavily barred than adult males.

Northern Pygmy-Owl

Glaucidium gnoma

L 6-7 | **WS** 13-13.5"

Oregon's smallest owl is diurnal, preying mostly on birds in broad daylight. Northern Pygmy-Owls are found commonly in the foothills and mid-elevations of nearly all of the state's mountain ranges. Whistled imitations of their evenly spaced hollow toots will not only bring in the occasional owl, but also gain the attention of chickadees, nuthatches, kinglets, and other small birds determined to keep a close eye on this small but fierce predator. Pygmy-owls often sit near the tip-top of the tallest tree in a forest opening, giving themselves an unrestricted view of their surroundings. Clear-cut openings and forests where there has been selective thinning are good places to look for this owl.

All ages similar. Small, round-headed owl with a conspicuous tail. Medium-brown head and upper parts. Underparts white with dense dark streaks. Markings on back of head look like a second set of eyes.

Burrowing Owl
Athene cunicularia

L 7.5–8 | **WS** 21.5"

The sight of a jay-sized owl standing upright on a fence post in the middle of the day is always surprising. Burrowing Owls occupy arid grasslands, disturbed rangelands, deserts, and drier agricultural fields, where they nest in abandoned mammals burrows. In eastern Oregon, old badger burrows with raised entrances are popular with this species, as their skirt of bare dirt makes it easy to spot approaching predators. Burrowing Owls have been steadily declining across their range for many decades, and they are now gone from the few westside sites where they once nested. A few winter annually the Willamette Valley, roosting in small concrete culverts at the edges of tilled fields. Male song is a quail- or dove-like *coo, HOO, hoo*. When startled or flushed, they give a raspy chatter.

Adult. Skinny, upright owl with longish unfeathered legs. Overall plumage warm sandy brown with extensive pale mottling. Distinctive whitish unibrow over wide-set pale yellow eyes.

Spotted Owl

Strix occidentalis

L 18.5-19 | **WS** 40"

Unfortunate victims of their own strict habitat requirements, Spotted Owls in their northern range almost exclusively inhabit the type of moist old-growth conifer forests that were systematically logged off during the mid-twentieth-century boom in Oregon's timber economy. These owls became the reviled poster child of a conservation movement that eventually led to the cessation of old-growth logging in the Coast and Cascade Ranges, but that alone may not save them: add in climate change and the continuing range expansion of the larger and more aggressive Barred Owl, and this species appears destined to become an owl without a forest. Barred Owls are known to kill or drive off Spotted Owls and to hybridize with them. The modest breeding population that survives is now confined to limited upslope stands where Barred Owls are absent. Call is a deep and resonant four-note series, *HOO, hoo-hoo, HOO.*

Adult. Large, round-headed owl. Plumage mostly dark brown with extensive creamy-white spotting above and below. White eyebrows above dark eyes.

Barred Owl

Strix varia

L 17-20 | **WS** 39-43"

Beginning in the mid-1970s, the Barred Owl has replaced and out-competed the Spotted Owl across much of its former range in the Coast and Cascades Ranges. Barred Owls now inhabit all of Oregon's heavily forested mountain ranges. Slightly larger and less habitat-specific than the Spotted Owl, they are well suited to take advantage of the patchwork of second-growth forests that now cover western Oregon's mid- to low-elevation slopes. They also thrive in more urban and suburban areas, where they are routinely photographed on fences and decks in residential areas. Their loud resonant *who cooks for you, who cooks for you alllll* calls can be heard up to half a mile.

Adult. Large, round-headed owl. Paler and sandier gray-brown than Spotted Owl. Streaked, not spotted, lower breast and belly. Crown, upper back, and upper breast heavily barred. Plainer face with no eyebrow markings.

Great Gray Owl

Strix nebulosa

L 24—33" | **WS** 54—60"

This massive, round-headed owl is mostly fluff and feathers, weighing roughly half as much as the shorter but much stouter Great Horned Owl. Great Gray Owls are locally uncommon residents around meadow openings in montane pine and fir forests, where they usually nest in the tops of old-growth snags. Their distribution across Oregon is patchy. Traditional strongholds include the eastern slope of the Cascades in southern Deschutes and northern Klamath Counties, a cluster of nesting pairs in the Spring Creek area in the Blue Mountains east of Pendleton, and regular sightings on the west slope of the Cascades east of Medford. Single Great Grays occasionally wander into the westside lowlands, but they are generally brief visitors. Call is a single resonant, up-slurred *wooo*.

Adult. Extremely large, round-headed owl. Cryptic plumage is a subtle mix of grays and brown, with fine barring on most feathers. Vermiculated gray face. Eyes dull yellow.

Long-eared Owl

Asio otus

L 14-16" | **WS** 35-39"

Long-eared Owls are generally secretive, strictly nocturnal birds, and their status is not well known in Oregon. They nest and roost in virtually impenetrable stands of pines and willows. Based on occasional discoveries of roosting birds, they are presumed to winter in the Willamette Valley, but are rarely detected even there. Nests are regularly reported along the Central Patrol Road at Malheur N.W.R., but searching for them is a challenging slog of many miles spent staring into dense willow tangles. They give a variety of indistinct hoots and screeches that are not readily identifiable as a particular species, or even an owl at all. A single low-pitched hoot is the most commonly heard call.

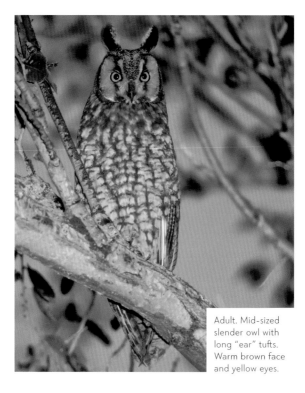

Adult. Mid-sized slender owl with long "ear" tufts. Warm brown face and yellow eyes.

Short-eared Owl

Asio flammeus

L 15" | **WS** 38"

This ground-dwelling owl with barely perceptible "ear" tufts is an uncommon nester in extensive grasslands across eastern Oregon. Short-eared Owls are found year-round in the Klamath, Summer Lake, and Harney Basins and around dryland wheat farms in Gilliam, Morrow, and Umatilla Counties. They are locally uncommon in winter in the western valleys and along the coast, when they roost communally with Northern Harriers and, occasionally, White-tailed Kites. As many as twenty owls have been counted at communal roosts in Linn and Lane Counties. Though sometimes active during the day, they usually leave roost sites shortly before dark, sometimes climbing a hundred feet or more into the air before flying off for a night's hunting. Their flight is butterfly-like, with deep wingbeats and erratic changes of direction. The perching posture is more horizontal than most owls. Typical call is a soft, raspy *skew.*

Adult. Mid-sized, long-winged owl with tiny, usually invisible "ear" tufts. Warm brown and buff overall, with heavily streaked underparts. Dark feathers accentuate the bright yellow eyes. In flight, a large dark patch on the upperwing and smaller dark patch on the underwing are conspicuous.

Northern Saw-whet Owl

Aegolius acadicus

L 7—8" | **WS** 16.5—18.5"

Perhaps the most widespread and abundant Oregon owl,
Northern Saw-whets are small, strictly nocturnal, and found
in dense woodlands, all of which contributes to making them
hard to see. Studies using mist nets have demonstrated that
they are highly migratory, even though some are found in many
areas year-round. They are generally cavity nesters, but to the
surprise of researchers, many pairs occupied and raised broods
in nest boxes put out for other species on a commercial poplar
farm in Morrow County. Common calls include a loud *skew* and
an incessant series of single high-pitched toots.

Adult. Small, plump, round-headed owl. Dark brown above. Large white spots on wings.
Broad white V-shaped eyebrow. Fine whitish streaking on head. Whitish underparts with
heavy brown streaking. Eyes yellow.

Belted Kingfisher

Megaceryle alcyon

L 13" | **WS** 20"

Kingfishers are colorful birds with comically oversized heads and bills, They are found around the glob, but the big, noisy Belted Kingfisher is the only member of the family to occur in Oregon. They are found statewide anywhere this is water with fish in it. Loud, ratcheting machine-gun-like calls announce their arrival. They can hover for many seconds with frenetic wingbeats before plunging into the water to capture prey, which includes small fish and tadpoles. They also sit on utility wires over the water. Nests are built in burrows they dig themselves, usually in the banks of small streams and rivers.

Adult female. Dark grayish-blue head and upperparts. Broad grayish-blue breast band, rusty belly band, and rusty flank. Underparts otherwise clean white. Huge head with shaggy crest and massive black bill. Adult male like female, but without rusty markings.

Lewis's Woodpecker

Melanerpes lewis

L 10.25-11" | **WS** 19.25-20.5"

Named for the famed explorer Meriwether Lewis, this woodpecker is unique in coloration and behavior. Unlike most other
woodpeckers, Lewis's Woodpeckers catch food on the wing,
making sudden flycatcher-like sallies to nab flying insects.
In extended flight, their deep, powerful wing beats are often
described as crow-like. They nest and winter in oak savanna
habitats, which have been largely converted to housing developments and vineyards across western Oregon. Hence, they
have disappeared from much of their historic breeding range.
They still breed in pockets of oak and pine on the east slope of
the Cascades and in river valleys in eastern Oregon. The Tygh
Valley area in Wasco County remains a stronghold of this beautiful woodpecker. Lewis's Woodpeckers are migratory, regularly
passing through Malheur N.W.R., and still occurring sporadically in the Willamette Valley in spring and fall. Not often
heard, the call is a series of grating *churr* notes.

Adult. Dark iridescent green
above with dark red.

Acorn Woodpecker

Melanerpes formicivorus

L 7.5-9" | **WS** 14-17"

The bright face pattern of this bird is suggestive of clown
makeup. Acorn Woodpeckers are almost always found in close
association with mature stands of oaks. Evidence of their presence comes in the form of "granaries," dead limbs or utility
poles riddled with holes stuffed with acorns. Unlike most
woodpeckers, Acorns are colonial, and they will gang up to
attack other woodpeckers that venture into their territory.
They inhabit all of the interior valleys of western Oregon, more
abundantly to the south in the Umpqua and Rogue Valleys.
The single colony east of the Cascades is at Running Y Ranch
north of Klamath Falls. They are loud and chatty, with the most
commonly heard call a dry *racka, racka, racka*.

Adult. Sexes nearly identical.
Sulfur-yellow to whitish face,
black hood and chin, white
eye, and bright red crown
create a unique head
pattern.

Williamson's Sapsucker

Sphyrapicus thyroideus

L 8.25–10" | **WS** 15.75"

Williamson's Sapsuckers are uncommon to common breeders in mixed conifer forests with ponderosa pine. They nest along the eastern slope of the Cascades and in all Oregon mountain ranges farther to the east. They rarely stray west of the Cascades. Nests are typically located in mature ponderosa pines or large ponderosa pine snags, and are normally at least thirty feet off the ground. Males and females differ more dramatically in appearance than do most woodpeckers. Stuttering *rat-a-tat* drum pattern is more protracted than those of other sapsuckers. Call is a harsh and explosive *quee-ah*, often in a series.

Adult female/immature. Densely barred blackish and white, looks gray at a distance. Extensive grocery sack-brown on the head. Yellow belly. Immature similar, but barring browner and buffier.

Adult male. Mostly black with red chin and narrow white head stripes. Rich lemon-yellow belly. Large white wing patch.

Red-naped Sapsucker

Sphyrapicus nuchalis

L 7.5-8.25" | **WS** 16-17"

Red-naped Sapsuckers nest along the eastern slope of the Cascades and in Oregon mountain ranges farther to the east, almost always in association with streamside aspens. They are short-distance migrants, mostly leaving the state during winter. Their breeding range overlaps extensively with that of the Red-breasted Sapsucker, and the two species hybridize frequently, producing offspring with a wide variety of intermediate plumages. Drum pattern is a steady *rrrat-a-tttat tat tat tat*. Call is a loud nasal *wah, wah, wah*, more hollow in tone than the calls of other sapsuckers.

Adult male. Solid red throat with incomplete black frame. Striking black and white head pattern. Red crown and red patch on nape. Adult female (not shown) similar to male, but with white chin.

Red-breasted Sapsucker

Sphyrapicus ruber

L 8-8.75" | **WS** 14.5-16"

This is Oregon's "red-headed" woodpecker, resident throughout most of western Oregon and along the east slope of the Cascades north of Klamath County, and in southwest Oregon and the southern Cascades east to at least the Warner Mountains. Red-naped and Red-breasted Sapsuckers often interbreed, creating hybrids that defy clear labels. Drum pattern is the most irregular and stuttering of the sapsuckers. This species will drum on anything that resonates, including metal light poles, gutters, and street signs. Call is a harsh, nasal *wee-ah*.

Adult. Males and females are similar, females averaging slightly duller. The extensively red head is unique among Oregon woodpeckers.

Downy Woodpecker

Dryobates pubescens

L 7" | **WS** 12"

The Downy Woodpecker is the smallest and most widespread Oregon woodpecker and the expected species at backyard feeders, where the eat suet and seed. Downy Woodpeckers are habitat generalists, found in almost any type of mid- to low-elevation woodland. Rapid staccato territorial drumming is usually performed on a dead tree limb. Calls include a single high-pitched, squeaky *peek*, also repeated to form an accelerating whinny.

Adult male. Small, sparrow-sized black and white woodpecker red nape patch. Stubby bill is about one-third the length of the head.

Adult female. Similar to male, but without red on head.

Hairy Woodpecker

Dryobates villosus

L 9" | **WS** 15"

Virtually identical in plumage to the smaller Downy, the Hairy Woodpecker tends to prefer forests with a conifer component, and is less likely to show up at a backyard feeder. Its drum pattern is even more rapid and less staccato than the Downy's. Call is a louder, more metallic *peek*. The rattle call is similar to the Downy's whinny, but more woody or hollow in tone, and lacks the smaller species' acceleration.

Adult male. Robin-sized black and white woodpecker with red nape patch. Longer bill is at least half the length of the head.

Adult female. Similar to male, but without red on head.

White-headed Woodpecker

Dryobates albolarvatus

L 8.25-9" | **WS** 16-17"

These stunning birds are uncommon residents along the eastern slope of the Cascades and in the Ochoco, Blue, Wallowa, and Warner Mountains. They are also uncommon breeders in the Siskiyou Mountains of southwest Oregon. White-headed Woodpeckers are ponderosa-pine obligates, rarely found away from mature stands of this species. Pine seeds make up a large part of their diet. Nest holes are usually in large ponderosa pine snags. Rapid staccato drum trails off at the end. Call is a dry, harsh *pit-it*. Rattle call is similar to that of Hairy Woodpecker.

Adult. Unmistakable, all-black woodpecker with white head. Only males have red nape patch.

American Three-toed Woodpecker

Picoides dorsalis

L 8" | **WS** 15"

Although resident and reasonably widespread, this is the hardest of Oregon's woodpeckers to find. Three-toeds inhabit higher elevations in the Cascades, Blue, and Wallowa Mountains, in the true fir zone between about 4,000 feet and timberline. They typically nest in live trees on the edges of stands with trees that have been killed by fire or insect damage. They tend to be most numerous and can be downright abundant in recently burned stands, with peak numbers present during the first two or three summers after a fire. Steady staccato drum trails off at the end. Call is a flat, slightly squeaky *pwik*. Rattle call is similar to that of Hairy Woodpecker, but more grating.

Adult male. Very similar to but smaller than Hairy Woodpecker. Golden-yellow crown patch. Dingier barred flanks. Female lacks yellow crown.

Black-backed Woodpecker

Picoides arcticus

L 9" | **WS** 16"

Black-backed Woodpeckers are among the first and most numerous species to occupy a forest in the wake of a fire. They are mostly found in lodgepole and ponderosa pine forests with lots of dead or dying trees, where they strip charred or dead bark off in large chunks as they hunt beetle larvae and other insects. Nest holes are usually in dead trees. They are uncommon to common in dry pine forests on the east slope of the Cascades and in other Oregon mountain ranges to the east, but rarely stray west of the Cascade Crest or into the lowlands. Steady staccato drum doesn't trail off at end. Call a loud, hollow *chek*. Distinctive rattle call is chattering, with an accelerated raspy ending.

Adult male. Similar in size and pattern to Hairy and American Three-toed Woodpeckers, but has only one white face stripe and a solid black back. Golden-yellow crown patch on male and immature only.

Northern Flicker

Colaptes auratus

L 12" | **WS** 20"

Lacking the black and white patterns of many other woodpeckers, flickers are large brown woodpeckers with colorful wings (red or, less frequently, yellow in Oregon) that routinely poke around on lawns and in the dirt in search of food. Individual flickers are migratory, but some are present statewide at any time of year. Calls include a piercing series of loud *yerk, yerk, yerk*... notes and a single nasal *skeeyu*.

Adult male Red-shafted. Large grayish to sandy-brown woodpecker, with long, pointed bill. Heavily black barring above. Extensive black spotting below. Black breast bib. Red jaw stripe. Orangish-red shafts in wing and tail feathers.

Adult male Yellow-shafted (rare). Same as Red-shafted, but with large red nape patch and black jaw stripe. Bright yellow shafts in wing and tail feathers.

Pileated Woodpecker

Dryocopus pileatus

L 16" | **WS** 29"

This is the largest and the only crested woodpecker north of Mexico. Everything about Pileated Woodpeckers is big and boisterous, from their loud staccato calls to their thunderous drumming. Most impressive is the ferocity with which they convert decaying snags into sawdust and mulch. It can make one's head hurt just watching a Pileated pound away at a tree stump. Huge nest holes are usually excavated fairly high in dead snags, and after the woodpeckers have abandoned them, are often used by other creatures including owls and squirrels. Their flight is less undulating than most woodpeckers' and is characterized by the distinct rowing motion of their deep and deliberate wing beats. Call is a sometimes lengthy series of loud *wuck, wuck, wucks* often given non-stop as they fly.

Adult. Unmistakable crow-sized black and white woodpecker, with bright red triangular crest. Male has red in jaw stripe, female does not.

American Kestrel

Falco sparverius

L 9" | **WS** 22"

Across much of Oregon, North America's smallest and most colorful falcon is one of the most likely birds to be seen on a utility wire. American Kestrels eat mainly small rodents, hovering for many seconds before dropping on the unsuspecting prey below and returning to a wire to eat. Their relaxed wing-beats look inefficient compared to the dashing flight styles of other falcons. Kestrels are cavity nesters, using natural cavities and old woodpecker holes in dead snags. They will also use nest boxes. Though they can be found anywhere in the state, they are most abundant in lowland open country. Populations are sparse along the outer coast and at higher elevations. Though the species is present in the state all year, some individual kestrels migrate. Frequently heard call is an insistent *killee, killee, killee*.

Adult male. Colorful and highly patterned. Crown and wings steely gray-blue. Back rich rusty brown with black barring. Black and white face. Heavily spotted underparts are buffy on breast, creamy white on belly and undertail. Rusty tail with black tip.

Adult female. Similar to adult male, but wings and back uniform reddish brown and barred. Tail duller rusty brown and finely barred throughout.

Merlin

Falco columbarius

L 10" | **WS** 24"

Only slightly larger than a kestrel, the Merlin is a different brand of falcon. It flies with incredible speed and purpose, rarely gliding or loafing along with lazy wingbeats. When hunting during winter, particularly in residential neighborhoods, Merlins assume sentinel perches in the tallest tree to survey the landscape for potential prey, which includes small to medium-sized birds. Once a victim is spotted, they attack, hitting top speed almost immediately. They take passerines and shorebirds right out of the air. During migration, Merlins move along in concert with flights of shorebirds and small land birds as if they were a rolling buffet. Migrants are most often encountered along the coast and at hawkwatch stations, such as Bonney Butte in Hood River County. Merlins are uncommon wintering birds statewide, mostly at lower elevations, and rare breeders in the Blue and Wallowa Mountains in northeast Oregon. They rarely vocalize away from breeding grounds.

Adult female flight. Females larger and broader-winged than males, but otherwise similar. Upper parts dark chocolate-brown instead of gray.

Adult male. Proportionally longer-winged and shorter-tailed than a kestrel. Flat crown, blocky head shape. Upperparts dark bluish-gray. Underparts creamy white with heavily streaked breast and barred belly and flanks. Tail mostly black with narrow white bars.

Peregrine Falcon
Falco peregrinus

L 16" | **WS** 41"

Considered the fastest-flying North American bird, the Peregrine Falcon is another species whose population rebounded after DDT was banned. Seeing a Peregrine is no longer a rare event in Oregon, and there are many breeding pairs, including at least one in downtown Portland. Nests are typically on cliff ledges and rocky outcrops, but sometimes on man-made structures such as tall buildings and bridges. Peregrines winter commonly along the coast and in the Willamette Valley and other sites where waterfowl are plentiful. They are decidedly less common east of the Cascades, especially during the winter months. Typical call is a rapid series of raspy, screeching *kak, kak, kak* notes.

Adult. Bluish-gray above and white below, with varying amounts of black barring on lower breast and belly. Black "helmet" with distinctive cheek mark. Bright yellow legs and feet. Yellow covering on nostrils.

Juvenile. Dark, dusky chocolate-brown above, creamy white below with heavy and dense dark brown streaking. Dull greenish-yellow legs. Gray covering on nostrils.

Prairie Falcon

Falco mexicanus

L 14.5–18.5" | **WS** 35.5–44.5"

This large falcon is an open-country denizen, favoring tree-less landscapes across the Great Plains and arid West. It is uncommon to common throughout Oregon's sagebrush steppe and in the treeless agricultural lands of the Mid-Columbia Basin. A few Prairie Falcons winter in the southern Willamette Valley, where expanses of cultivated grassland mimic their preferred habitat. They also winter sparingly in the Rogue Valley. Nesting occurs on rimrock ledges throughout south-eastern Oregon, but Prairie Falcons do not breed west of the Cascades. Fort Rock, in northern Lake County, is a great place to see this species, as there is always a pair nesting somewhere on the volcanic neck. The drive along U.S. Highway 20 between Bend and Burns is also good for Prairie Falcons, often spotted on roadside utility poles. Vocalizations include an accelerating agitated *kik, kik, kik, kik* alarm call and a protracted, wavering *eeech* call given by courting adults.

Adult perched. Sexes similar, with females larger and broader-winged than males. Upperparts earthy dirt-brown. Underparts white, with crisp dark breast streaks and broader streaking towards lower flank. Face pattern includes pale eyeborw and narrow brownish cheek marking.

Adult flight. In flight, the "wingpits" and wing linings are extensively black.

Olive-sided Flycatcher

Contopus cooperi

L 7-8 | **WS** 13"

Like their close pewee relatives, Olive-sided Flycatchers love high exposed perches from which to chase passing insects. Olive-sideds are found throughout Oregon from May to August. They are uncommon breeders in all of the state's mountain ranges, normally on mid- to low-elevation forested slopes with openings, where they hunt from the tops of the tallest dead trees. The well-known mnemonic for their emphatic, three-note whistled song is *quick, three beers*. Call is a quickly whistled *pip, pip, pip*.

Adult. Large angular head and bill. Wings long, extending nearly to the tip of the tail. Upperparts solid dark olive-brown. Diffuse wing bars. Throat whitish. Dark "vest" on breast and flanks is noticeably streaked, divided down the center by creamy white.

Western Wood-Pewee
Contopus sordidulus

L 5.5–6.25 | **WS** 10"

Occasionally mistaken for one of the smaller, more greenish
Empidonax flycatchers, Western Wood-Pewees differ in their
habit of making extended flights in pursuit of insect prey,
usually returning to the same favored high perch over and over
again. Although they may be found at higher elevations, wood-
pewees are predominantly lowland birds, commonest in the tall
cottonwood forests along major rivers. As in most flycatchers,
voice is the best means of identification. The song is a quick,
soft stuttering *lllive a bit*, followed by a lazily whistled
pee-eerrr. The common call note is a plaintive single-note
whistle, *peee*.

Adult. Angular head with peaked hind crown. Dark, dusky
olive-brown above. Soft wing bars. No eye ring. Long primaries
extend halfway down tail. Underparts pale grayish, with darker
olive-gray "vest." Lower belly and undertail slightly yellowish.

Willow Flycatcher

Empidonax traillii

L 5.25–6.75 | **WS** 7.5–9.5"

The largest of Oregon's Empidonax flycatchers is differs from the others in its poorly defined wing bars and the absence of a clear eye ring. As its name suggests, this species has a preference for riparian bottomlands dominated by willows. It's hard to imagine that any place on Earth has a higher density of breeding Willow Flycatchers than Central Patrol Road at Malheur N.W.R. After driving the southernmost ten miles of this road along a willow-lined canal, it can feel like you have encountered more Willow Flycatchers than mosquitoes. Other favored habitats include regenerating clearcuts with short alders, willows, and Douglas-fir saplings; such patches are widespread in the Coast Range and in the western foothills of the Cascades. The readily identifiable, raspy *fitz-bew* song is easily heard in such places. The call note is a soft, liquid *whit*.

Adult. Entirely brown to olive-brown above. No eye ring. Diffuse buffy wing bars. Grayish to grayish olive breast. Belly and undertail pale sulfur-yellow. Slightly darker sides of breast may create slight "vest." Bill long and fairly heavy. Orangish-yellow lower bill, upper bill dark.

Hammond's Flycatcher

Empidonax hammondii

L 5–5.75 | **WS** 8.75"

One of three similar olive and gray Empidonax flycatchers
with crisp wing bars and complete eye rings found in Oregon
from mid-April to late September, Hammond's Flycatchers nest
commonly in most of the state's mountains ranges both east
and west of the Cascades, primarily in wetter mid-elevation
conifer forests. It is absent as a breeder in the arid southeastern corner of Oregon. This is Oregon's smallest and most
frenetic flycatcher, habitually flicking its wings and flipping
its tail simultaneously. Hammond's Flycatchers nest and feed
fairly high, generally inside the tree canopy and often thirty
feet or more off the ground. On cold days during migration,
they may be seen lower. Song has two phrases, a high-pitched
and up-slurred *see-bit* followed by a burry *rrrup*. Call note is a
sharply whistled *peep*.

Adult. Head proportionally
large, with squared-off hind
crown. All-dark bill short and
thin with nail-like tip. Tail short.
Long primary projection. Eye
ring expanded into a
"teardrop" behind eye.

Gray Flycatcher

Empidonax wrightii

L 5.5–6.25 | **WS** 8.75"

The Gray is the largest of the three similar olive and gray Empidonax flycatchers with crisp wing bars and complete eye rings found in Oregon from mid-April to late September. It is also the longest-tailed and longest-billed of the three. Breeding almost exclusively east of the Cascades, Grays nest in big sagebrush and in arid pine and juniper forests with sage understory. They perch five or six feet off the ground, then drop down to grab insects. This species distinctively wags the tail slowly downwards rather than flipping it up like other Empidonax; wing flicking is infrequent. The song comprises two phrases, an upslurred, slightly grating *ch-lip* followed by a downslurred, slightly grating *ch-lup*. Call a crisply whistled *prit* or *pit*.

Adult. Long, narrow tail. Longish bill dark above and mostly orangish-yellow below. Medium primary projection beyond secondaries. Thin eye ring.

Dusky Flycatcher

Empidonax oberholseri

L 5.25-6 | **WS** 8-9"

One of three similar olive and gray Empidonax flycatchers with crisp wing bars and complete eye rings found in Oregon from mid-April to late September, the Dusky Flycatcher breeds in mixed conifer and deciduous woodland, often around seasonally wet meadows or riparian corridors. A widespread nester east of the Cascades crest and in the mountains of southwest Oregon, it is absent from the Coast Range and Willamette Valley except as a scarce spring migrant. Typically perches within twenty-five feet of the ground on exterior branches. The tail movements can be confusing, as the tail is often quickly flipped up and then slowly lowered, inviting confusion with the Gray Flycatcher; rarely, it also flips the tail and flicks the wings simultaneously like the Hammond's Flycatcher. The song is a combination of three distinct phrases, not always given in the same order: a rising *pri-lit*, usually followed by a lower-pitched burry *prrreet*, and ending with a clear, thin *seet*. Calls include a soft flat *whit* and a plaintive whistled *dew-hic* or *dew, dew-hic*.

Adult. Medium-sized to smallish head with domed crown. Medium-length, narrow tail. Bill longer than in Hammond's and shorter than in Gray, dark above and yellow below. Eye ring evenly thick throughout, pale patch between eye and bill. Short primary projection.

Pacific-slope Flycatcher

Empidonax difficilis

L 5.5-6.75 | **WS** 8-9"

Two nearly identical Empidonax species, both the Pacific-slope Flycatcher and the Cordilleran Flycatcher are presumed to breed in Oregon, but telling these two species apart is difficult even by voice. The Pacific-slope is generally accepted to be the breeding bird in the Coast Range, westside lowlands, and Cascades, but the identity of the birds nesting in more easterly mountain ranges remains a source of confusion and debate. Pacific-slope Flycatchers arrive in April throughout western Oregon ,where they breed in wetter drainages from the valley floor to around 3,000 feet. Their song is a high-pitched *pseet, tsick, seet*. Calls include the commonly heard *peer-wheet*, like a whistle to get your attention, and the less common and almost inaudible metallic *tink*, generally given in migration.

Adult. Peaked hind crown. Rich leaf-green above and yellowish below. Sides of upper breast olive-green, creating "vested" loook.

Black Phoebe

Sayornis nigricans

L 6.25 | **WS** 11"

Black Phoebes nest uncommonly throughout most of western Oregon's lowlands, with a few found each year east of the Cascades. Resident in all coastal counties, they are particularly abundant in coastal Coos and Curry Counties and fairly common in the Rogue and Umpqua Valleys. They remain scarce in the northern Willamette Valley, but are uncommon breeders from Corvallis south. They also occur regularly in southern Klamath County and sporadically along the Blitzen River near Frenchglen in Harney County. Usually seen actively pumping their tail, Black Phoebes are almost always found near water, nesting under bridges and natural overhangs along small streams, rivers, and wooded ponds and sloughs. A high-pitched, sharply whistled *tseep* is the most commonly heard vocalization.

Adult. Distinctive medium-sized flycatcher with peaked hind crown and long, narrow tail. Head, breast, and upperparts black. Belly and undertail white. All-dark bill.

Say's Phoebe

Sayornis saya

L 6.75 | **WS** 13"

One of the first spring migrant land birds to arrive east of the Cascades, the charming and confiding Say's Phoebe normally reaches southeastern Oregon by late February. They inhabit nearly all of the eastside lowlands, particularly more arid areas. They occur annually west of the Cascades, mostly as overshoots in March and early April. A few overwinter each year in the Rogue, Umpqua, and Willamette Valleys, and sometimes in the pasturelands of northern Curry County. These hardy birds build their nests in barns and sheds and under the eaves of houses, sometimes within a few feet of busy human pathways. Typical call is a clear whistled *pee-urr*, slightly upslurred.

Adult. Peaked hind crown. Fairly long, squared-off tail. Back, wings, and tail earth-brown. Very subtle wing bars. Throat buffy-gray, breast pale sandy-brown. Belly and undertail salmon-orangish, sometimes looking a bit yellowish. Short, thin bill.

Ash-throated Flycatcher

Myiarchus cinerascens

L 7.5–8.5 | **WS** 11.75–15.5"

This large, upright, slightly crested and long-tailed flycatcher breeds in dry canyons and on arid foothill slopes. West of the Cascades, Ash-throated Flycatchers are confined to the foothills of the Rogue Valley, where they nest in scrubby oaks with California lilac understory. Occasional strays wander to similar habitats in the Umpqua and Willamette Valleys. In the Columbia Gorge, Ash-throateds are locally common in steep, oak-filled draws around Mosier and The Dalles. The also inhabit the juniper belt running through the middle of state in the rain shadow of the Cascades. In the arid south-eastern quadrant of Oregon, Ash-throated Flycatchers breed in canyons, dry or with permanent streams, filled with juniper, box elder, chokecherry, and occasional cottonwoods. They are generally absent from northeastern Oregon. Common vocalizations include a soft, throaty *ka-brick* and a louder, raspier *chick-wheer*.

Adult. Mostly warm brown above, with rustier crown, tail, and wings. Wing coverts and secondaries with pale edges. Throat and breast pale ash-gray. Belly and undertail pale sulfur-yellow. All-dark bill.

Tropical Kingbird

Tyrannus melancholicus

L 7-9 | **WS** 15-16"

Tropical Kingbird is one of several southerly flycatchers prone to "reverse migration," going north in the autumn when they should be moving south. Oregon averages ten to twnety Tropical Kingbird sightings per fall, mostly along the outer coast during October and November, a month or more after our Eastern and Western Kingbirds have left for the winter. A few Tropicals linger into December. These strays are mostly immature birds, migrating for the first time. Similar in habits to Western Kingbirds, Tropicals are found in semi-open country and pastures, where they perch on fences or utility wires. Call is a long, slightly upslurred trill, not often heard in Oregon.

Immature. More extensively yellow below and greener on the back than similar Western Kingbird. Longer, thicker dark bill. Tail lacks white outer edges and is slightly notched.

Western Kingbird

Tyrannus verticalis

L 8-9.5 | **WS** 14.5-15.75"

The expected kingbird in Oregon during the breeding season,
Western Kingbirds are fearless, with "fight" always trumping
"flight" in the face of danger. They arrive in the state in mid-
to late April and leave by late August, shortly after young are
fledged and independent. They prefer open country, and thus
are most abundant in arid areas east of the Cascades, particularly southeastern Oregon. On the westside, they nest commonly
in the Rogue and Umpqua Valleys, are uncommon breeders
in the southern Willamette Valley, and only occasionally nest
north of about Salem. During spring migration, fair numbers
of Westerns appear in coastal pastures, but none remain to nest
there. The untidy nests are often built on utility pole crossbars
and transformers. Vocalizations are a mix of sputtering squeaky
twitters and sharp *kip* notes.

Adult. Gray and olive-green
above. Pale ash-gray throat and
upper breast. Lower breast,
belly, and undertail rich lemon
yellow. Medium-length black tail
with white outer edges.

Eastern Kingbird
Tyrannus tyrannus

L 7.5–9 | **WS** 13–15"

Arriving in early May and departing in by September, Eastern
Kingbirds are uncommon to common breeders along eastern
and central Oregon's major rivers and their tributaries,
including the Deschutes, John Day, Umatilla, and Grande
Ronde. These black and white flycatchers are also readily
found along the Blitzen River, which runs through the center
of Malheur N.W.R. Like all kingbirds, Easterns are fearless in
the face of danger. Territorial birds often perch prominently at
the tops of bushes and low trees. They can also be seen on low
branches over water when they are feeding. Song is a sputtering
series of rising notes following by a buzzy, slurred *zeer*. Call a
loud metallic *tsee*, sometimes repeated.

Adult. Robin-sized
flycatcher, predominantly
black and slate-gray
above and white below.
Conspicuous white tip on
tail. Medium-sized,
all-dark bill.

Loggerhead Shrike

Lanius ludovicianus

L 8-9 | **WS** 11-12.5"

Shrikes are songbirds with bad intentions. They use their strong hooked beak to kill small birds and rodents, often impaling their meal on a thorn or barbed wire before eating it. The Loggerhead Shrike is the only species that breeds in Oregon; a few also overwinter. Loggerheads are common breeders across the open sagebrush steppe of southeastern Oregon. Their range also stretches north through the broad dry juniper belt and onto the Columbia Plateau in the rainshadow of the Cascades. They are rare but annual strays west of the Cascades. Song is a series of widely spaced vireo-like phrases. Call is a raspy scolding note.

Adult. Slender gray and black bird with short, thick, hooked beak. Upperparts darker gray than underparts. Black wings and tail. Black mask connects over the base of the bill. Flight is direct, with very rapid wingbeats. Conspicuous white wing patches.

Northern Shrike
Lanius excubitor

L 9-9.5 | **WS** 12-13.75"

Larger and paler than the Loggerhead, the Northern Shrike is
Oregon's expected winter shrike. Northerns arrive in October
and depart by early April. They are uncommon in the westside
valleys, and only slightly more usual across the northern tier
counties east of the Cascades. Oregon is near the southern edge
of the winter range, and Northern Shrikes are scarcer near the
California and Nevada borders. Open fields with brush or scattered small trees for hunting perches are the favored habitat.
Prey includes small birds and rodents; like other shrikes,
they may impale their meal on thorns or barbed wire before
consuming it. Most of the state's wintering Northerns are first-
winter birds with a fair amount of brown barring. They rarely
vocalize on the wintering grounds.

Immature. Conspicuous white wing
patch. First-winter birds are dingy
brownish-gray with fine brown barring
below. Black mask narrower than
adult's, sometimes nearly absent. Less
frequently seen adult is paler gray
than Loggerhead, with narrow mask
that does not connect over the base
of the bill. Flight is less direct and
more undulating than Loggerhead's.

Hutton's Vireo

Vireo huttoni

L 4-4.75 | **WS** 8.25"

Oregon's smallest and only year-round resident vireo is often confused with the Ruby-crowned Kinglet. Compared with the kinglet and other small songbirds, though, Hutton's Vireos are sluggish, stopping to look both ways and swiveling their heads to look some more before moving on. Rare strays east of the Cascades, they are uncommon to common in mid- to low-elevation mixed woodlands throughout western Oregon, including the coastal slope; numbers are higher in the Rogue and Umpqua Valley foothills than in the Willamette Basin or along the coast. They are most abundant in foothill areas with a diverse mix of cedars, Douglas-fir, oaks, madrone, and big leaf maple. Common call is a loud, repetitive *zooweep*. They also give a harsh scolding note.

Adult. Dull olive-green, with crisp cream-colored wing bars and thick, slightly hooked bill. Messy eye ring and pale lores. Feet bluish gray.

Cassin's Vireo

Vireo cassinii

L 4.5–5.5 | **WS** 9.5"

Cassin's Vireos arrive during early April in western Oregon, where they nest uncommonly at mid-elevations in the Coast Range and on the western slopes of the Cascades. They are more abundant in the mixed pine and fir woodlands east of the Cascades crest, where arrival is in early May. Cassin's Vireos also nest commonly at mid-elevations in the Blue, Ochoco, and Wallowa Mountains. Fall migration extends into early October, and there are even a few winter records. They move sluggishly and stay high in the canopy, where they are often first detected by their song, a set of widely spaced, burry two-note phrases that are repeated over and over. They also have a harsh scolding call.

Spring adult. Mostly olive-green above, with grayer head. Bold white eye ring and "spectacle." Indistinct wing bars. Variable yellow wash on flanks and vent. Fall birds in fresh plumage are more colorful and contrasting, with more prominent wing bars. Stubby, all-dark bill.

Warbling Vireo

Vireo gilvus

L 4.75–5 | **WS** 8.75"

The spiraling song of Warbling Vireos is an undeniable sign that spring has arrived. They are abundant spring migrants state-wide, arriving west of the Cascades about the third week of April and passing through central and eastern Oregon beginning in early May. They are common nesters in deciduous and mixed woodlands statewide, most common in riparian corridors and riverside forests with extensive cottonwoods. They are also abundant in low- to mid-elevation alder stands in the Coast Range and on the western slopes of the Cascades. Fall migration is protracted, with southbound birds still moving through into early October; none winter in Oregon. Song is a rapid up and down warble, the call a raspy scolding.

Adult. Dull olive above with grayish crown. Underparts off-white, with variable pale yellow wash on lower flanks; fresh fall birds yellower below. Poorly defined whitish eyebrow, diffuse dark line through the eye. Thick, medium-length bill.

Red-eyed Vireo
Vireo olivaceus

L 5 | **WS** 9-10"

Unseen Red-eyed Vireos sing their incessant chant from high in dense foliage, a tantalizing *see me, here I am, over here, see me, here I am, over here....* Aside from occasional migrants passing through Harney County oases, Red-eyed Vireos are found almost exclusively in gallery forests along the Columbia and Willamette Rivers. There is suitable habitat all along the Willamette River between Portand and Eugene. Sandy River Delta Park just east of Troutdale is the most reliable spot in Oregon to hear and see this species; Elijah Bristow State Park southeast of Eugene is another dependable site.

Adult. Large, long-billed vireo with olive-green back and whitish underparts. Crown bluish-gray narrowly edged black; dark eye line accentuates the whitish eyebrow. Red eye.

Canada Jay
Perisoreus canadensis

L 11.5" | **WS** 18"

Canada Jays (once called Gray Jays) are uncommon to common year-round residents of most of the state's mountains ranges. These tame birds frequently descend on campgrounds, hoping to score a handout or purloin a snack from the picnic table. The rustling of a potato chip bag is sure to bring them quietly gliding in. They typically reside at higher elevations in moist conifer woodlands, but are found near sea level on the outer coast. Birds in the Siskiyous and the Coast and Cascade Ranges show more extensive black on the crown than those in the Blues and Wallowas.

Coastal adult. Large and fluffy, with long, broad tail and short bill. This coastal adult has extensively black crown. Juvenile (below). Uniformly dark sooty-gray. Bill pink at base, bluish-gray in the middle and dark-tipped. Whitish tip to otherwise dark tail.

Pinyon Jay
Gymnorhinus cyanocephalus

L 10.25–11.5" | **WS** 18"

Nomadic and unpredictable, Pinyon Jays spend most of the year in large flocks roaming the mixed pine-juniper woodlands of central Oregon. The area around Cabin Lake Guard Station north of Fort Rock in Lake County has traditionally been the best place to look for this bird; flocks of up to 500 Pinyon Jays have been seen here. Their diverse diet includes nuts and seeds, insects, and even young birds. Call is a crow-like *caw*.

Adult. Fairly large, crow-shaped jay. Entirely grayish-blue plumage. Long, pointed black bill.

Steller's Jay
Cyanocitta stelleri

L 12–13.5" | **WS** 17.25"

This noisy, conspicuously crested jay is resident in forested areas statewide, but generally absent from the treeless Columbia Plateau and sagebrush steppe of southeastern Oregon. These jays are non-migratory, but move downslope in winter and upslope during the nesting season. Steller's Jays in the Cascades and western Oregon have light blue eyebrows, where those in the northeastern mountains have white. Standard calls include a loud staccato *shook, shook, shook*, and a more metallic and squeaky *sheek, sheek, sheek*.

Adult Coastal. Dark blue, with blackish head and crest. Wings and tail brighter blue, wth black bars. Eyebrow pale blue (adult interior white).

California Scrub-Jay

Aphelocoma californica

L 11-12" | **WS** 15.5"

Opportunistic and omnivorous, California Scrub-Jays Jays flourish in lowlands around human habitation, reaching their highest densities in semi-urban and suburban settings, where they often eat pet food and other foods that humans unintentionally make available. Many towns in the Mid-Columbia Basin and much of southeastern and central Oregon have thriving populations. A loud, repetitive, scratchy *schhenk* is the most frequent vocalization.

Adult. Slender, long-tailed jay. Azure-blue head, wings, and tail. Mantle gray. Underparts white to pale gray. Partial breast band is blue. Heavy black bill. Juvenile similar but mostly gray on head, nape, back, and breast band; shorter bill with pale base.

Clark's Nutcracker

Nucifraga columbiana

L 10.5–12" | **WS** 22"

Clark's Nutcrackers, named for the explorer William Clark, reside in subalpine habitats all along the crest of the Cascades, and are also common at higher elevations in the Ochoco, Blue and Wallowa Mountains. Most frequently found near timberline, they also descend into the ponderosa and lodgepole pine belts as they cache food for winter. Timberline Lodge on Mt. Hood and Crater Lake National Park are reliable places to see this engaging and curious bird. Like Canada Jays, they visit campsites and picnic tables looking for easy snacks. Nutcrackers have a remarkable ability to memorize the location of their stashes of nuts and seeds, letting them find them again many months later in the winter. A grating, slightly nasal *karack* is the typical call.

Adult. Nearly crow-sized. Mostly pale gray with broad, rounded black wings and tail, which show extensive white in flight. Long pointed bill.

Black-billed Magpie
Pica hudsonia

L 17.75-23.75" | **WS** 22-24"

Conspicuous and unmistakable, the extremely intelligent
Black-billed Magpie is also a bit larcenous, making off with any
food treasures that humans happen to leave unattended. Often
traveling in noisy flocks, these social birds are uncommon
to common in cultivated valleys and riparian corridors
throughout central and eastern Oregon, but occur only as
wanderers west of the Cascades. Although they are often found
on the fringes of human settlements, they are wary of humans
after centuries of persecution and do not usually visit residential areas like other crows and jays. Their large stick nests are
usually in dense willows near water. Vocalizations include a
harsh, raspy *wawk, wawk, wawk* and a thin, nasal *weer*.

Adult. Black and
white, with highly
iridescent wings and
long tail. Black bill.

American Crow

Corvus brachyrhynchos

L 17" | **WS** 39"

Though the American Crow seems to be a constant presence, in Oregon this species is rarely found far from human habitation and cultivated areas. Crows are permanent residents throughout western Oregon's lowland valleys, foothills, and coastal slope; their distribution is patchier east of the Cascades, and they are scarce to absent across most of southeastern Oregon, where they are replaced by the more hardy Common Raven. They are present in numbers in the heavily cultivated lowlands of the Snake and Columbia Rivers. Crows withdraw from some areas in harsh winters. Highly social, American Crows may have as many as 250 different vocalizations, the most common of which is a loud and persistent *caw*.

Flight. Medium-length wings are broad, with rounded tips. Tail tip is square or slightly rounded. Head barely projects in front of the wing. Wingbeats somewhat floppy. Adult. Large all-black bird with sturdy bill. Slightly iridescent wings.

Common Raven

Corvus corax

L 22—27" | **WS** 45—46.5"

Larger and more rural in distribution than the American Crow, Common Ravens are hardy and resourceful, capable of enduring much harsher winter conditions than most birds. They are most abundant away from human habitation. Ravens inhabit rural and montane areas statewide, including the outer coast, and are the default large black bird of montane areas and the expansive sagebrush steppe of southeastern Oregon, where crows are wholly or mostly absent. Once absent from the Portland Metro area, ravens are now of uncommon occurrence there, perhaps the result of less human persecution. They place their large stick nests in tall trees and on power poles and rimrock ledges. During the nesting season, ravens routinely raid the nests of other birds for eggs and nestlings. Call is a loud, croaking *wock*.

Flight. Style is more powerful and efficient than a crow's, and wingbeats are shallower. Wings often look crooked or slightly swept back. Longer head and neck projection in front of wings. Wedge-shaped tail. Adult. Larger and longer-billed than the American Crow.

Horned Lark

Eremophila alpestris

L 7" | **WS** 12"

Horned Larks are common to abundant throughout the
Columbia Plateau and the southeastern Oregon sagebrush
country and on open fields and grasslands in northeastern
Oregon and the Snake River basin. They also nest on many
peaks in the Cascades and on Steens Mountain. The critically
threatened "Streaked" population (subspecies) of the Horned
Lark has dwindled to less than 2000 individuals in the central
Willamette Valley, but other populations of this widespread
species are thriving across the eastern two-thirds of Oregon.
Males circle high overhead while singing their ascending
warble of tinkling notes. Common call is *see dirt*.

Adult male. Mostly pale sandy-
brown above and white below.
Throat and breast vary from yellow
to white. Black bib, black and white
face with black crown feathers
sticking up like horns. Rare and
declining "Streaked" Horned Lark
adult is darker and more colorful,
with streaked upper breast.

Adult female. Less contrastingly patterned than male and lacks "horns." Female larks construct nests on bare ground weaving together grasses and other plants.

Juvenile. Mottled and scaled above, with plain face and streaked upper breast.

Purple Martin

Progne subis

L 8" | **WS** 16"

Our largest swallow is a locally uncommon breeder along the coast and throughout the interior valleys of western Oregon. Martins nest colonially, typically near water. There are several colonies along the Columbia River between Astoria and Hood River and south through the Willamette Valley, and nest boxes installed around most Oregon estuaries are also usually occupied. A pair or two nest in isolated snags at sites high in the Coast Range and on the west slope of the Cascades. They are absent farther east along the Columbia and rare elsewhere east of the Cascades. Martins feed high in the sky, their flight more direct and less buoyant than that of the smaller swallows and including prolonged glides. The loud chirping and chortling calls may be heard even when the birds are so high that they can't be seen.

Adult male. Entirely dark iridescent bluish-purple.

Adult female. Mostly dark above, with subtle iridescent purple on crown, back, and wings. Nape and forehead medium-gray. Underparts paler gray. Immature like female, but entirely dusky-brown above.

Tree Swallow

Tachycineta bicolor

L 6" | **WS** 14"

Tree Swallows return to western Oregon as early as late January, and are also among the earliest of our swallows to leave after nesting, typically hard to find after July. Tree Swallows are abundant nesters in tree cavities and nest boxes at wooded wetlands, ponds and lakes, and other waterways statewide, from sea level up to high mountain lakes. Flight is buoyant and graceful, with fluid wingbeats. Calls are throaty and gurgling.

Adult male. Stunningly dark iridescent greenish-blue above, gleaming white below. Break between blue and white on face runs below eye. Long dusky-brown wings extend to tip of tail. Dusky-brown tail slightly notched.

Female/immature. Adult female green or blue above, immature browner; white below. Dusky wash across immature's breast can look like a complete breast band.

Violet-green Swallow

Tachycineta thalassina

L 5" | **WS** 10.5"

Small and colorful, Violet-greens are Oregon's most urban
swallow. They generally arrive about two weeks after Tree
Swallows, and by late March their chatter fills the air over
residential neighborhoods and other heavily developed areas,
from sea level to timberline. They commonly nest under eaves
and on commercial buildings, where any cavity or vent provides
a potential nest site. Away from urban areas, they routinely
nest high on rimrocks and cliff faces, where they may share
the skies with White-throated Swifts and Cliff Swallows. They
feed higher in the sky than other swallows, on stiff, shallow,
fluttering wingbeats; their less fluid flight style can make them
seem more similar to swifts than to other swallows when seen
in silhouette. Call is a chattering *chee, chee, chee,* with other
twittering notes interspersed.

Flight. Only Oregon swallow with white
wrapping onto the side of the rump.
Comparatively short, broad-based wings;
short, slightly notched tail.

Adult. Bright emerald-green crown, nape, and
back. Rump vibrant purple and blue with
narrow white central stripe. Dusky brown
wings. Clean white below. White extends high
on the face, wrapping behind and slightly
above the eye.

Northern Rough-winged Swallow

Stelgidopteryx serripennis

L 5.5" | **WS** 11"

The brown-backed Northern Rough-winged Swallow is the least abundant of Oregon's swallows. It arrives quietly in early March, often going unnoticed in the feeding swarms dominated by Tree and Violet-green Swallows. A statewide breeder, it usually nests singly or in small groups in holes in river banks or road cuts Call is a burry throaty *churt*.

Flight. Proportionally long-winged and slight-bodied, this species has a fluid flight style.

Adult. Uniformly dirt-brown above, with minimal contrast between the back and upperwing. Throat and breast washed pale sandy-brown. Lower breast, belly, and undertail off-white. Eye surrounded by dark feathering.

Bank Swallow

Riparia riparia

L 5" | **WS** 13"

Smaller and more gregarious than the less common Northern Rough-winged, the Bank Swallow is Oregon's only swallow with a complete breast band. Bank Swallows breed in colonies sometimes numbering into the hundreds, riddling old old quarry faces, road cuts, and stream banks with their nest holes. Sites may be used for years, then be abruptly abandoned when a colony moves. Traditionally more common as a breeder east of the Cascades, Bank Swallows have established several westside colonies over the past decade, including one at Barton Park along the Clackamas River and another near Prescott in Columbia County. They are now regularly found in flocks of migrating swallows in the Willamette Valley and along the coast. Flight is more stiff-winged, fluttering, and frenetic than that of the Northern Rough-winged Swallow. Harsh call is often interspersed with high-pitched twitters.

Adult. Brown above and white below. Broad brown breast band contrasts with white throat, lower breast, and belly.

Flight. Stubby, broad-based wings and short, slightly notched tail.

Cliff Swallow

Petrochelidon pyrrhonota

L 5.5" | **WS** 11"

The compact, blunt-winged Cliff Swallow is an abundant breeder statewide, with the largest Oregon colonies normally found east of the Cascades. Cliff Swallows nest around many of the outbuildings and under most bridges at Malheur N.W.R., and they are equally abundant elsewhere in southeastern Oregon. Their massive colonies of adobe-like mud nests are constructed under the eaves of houses, sheds, and bridges, and on cliff faces. When a colony is approached, adults often pour out en masse with a hail of squeaky, grating chatter. When undisturbed, each nest entrance will be filled with the dark face and white forehead of an adult. The wingbeats tend to be stiffer and more rapid than those of other swallows. Common call is a piercing, nasal *chur*.

Adult. Chestnut face, white forehead, and orangish-buff rump. Crown and back dark blue. Wings dark dusky-brown. Buffy breast and flanks, belly and undertail off-white.

Flight. Thick body, short blunt wings, short square tail. Buffy rump. Rapid, fluttery wingbeats.

Barn Swallow

Hirundo rustica

L 7" | **WS** 12"

Worldwide in distribution, the sleek, long-winged and long-tailed Barn Swallow has a powerful but graceful flight style that makes it instantly recognizable in a mixed flock. Barn Swallows arrive in Oregon in late March and typically depart by early October. Recently they have frequently appeared in Oregon during midwinter, sometimes lingering for a week or two before disappearing. Barn Swallows breed statewide in habitats that range from urban to entirely rural. They nest as single pairs, placing their nests of mud and grass on the sides of buildings with overhangs that protect the nest and its contents from predators the elements. Almost any rural or semi-rural outbuilding or barn is likely to have a nesting pair. Highly varied vocalizations include complicated warbles and twitters along with a *cheep cheep* flight call.

Adult male. Iridescent blue crown and back. Forehead and chin dark rusty-brown. Underparts paler rust. Long, narrow wings; forked tail with long streamers and band of white spot. Female similar to male, but creamy white below.

Black-capped Chickadee
Poecile atricapillus

L 5–6 | **WS** 6–8"

This small black and white songbird with a distinctive song is a familiar feeder bird across much of North America. In Oregon, Black-capped Chickadees are common along the coast and throughout the interior valleys and associated foothills west of the Cascades, but have only a limited distribution in eastern Oregon. They are found in the Snake River basin in the lowland riparian corridors along the Deschutes, John Day, and Umatilla Rivers and their tributaries, but are wholly absent from most of southeastern Oregon. Black-capped Chickadees nest in natural tree cavities, old woodpecker holes, and man-made boxes. Song is a clearly whistled *fee-bee*. They respond readily to owl imitations and "pishing" sounds with vigorous scolding that often attracts a large mixed flock of other passerines.

Adult. Distinctive black cap and throat separated by a white cheek. Upperparts medium gray, pale pearly-gray below.

Mountain Chickadee

Poecile gambeli

L 4.75-5.5 | **WS** 8.25"

This species is found in all of Oregon's major mountains except for the Coast Range, most abundantly in lodgepole and ponderosa pine forests and less commonly in true fir and spruce forests closer to timberline. They are more common on the eastern slope of the Cascades than west of the crest; they occasionally stray to the outer coast. In some falls or winters, Mountain Chickadees descend into the lowlands in numbers, often appearing at bird feeders near the valley floor. They are otherwise non-migratory. Call suggests a Black-capped Chickadee with laryngitis, a raspier version of *chick-a-dee-dee-dee*.

Adult. Similar to Black-capped Chickadee, but with diagnostic white eyebrow and black stripe through the eye. Paler gray above than Black-capped.

Chestnut-backed Chickadee

Poecile rufescens

L 4-4.75 | **WS** 7.5"

Aside from an isolated population in the eastern Blue and
Wallowa Mountains, small and colorful Chestnut-backed
Chickadees in Oregon are found only from the crest of the
Cascades west. Most abundant in the Coast Range and at mid-
elevations on the west slope of the Cascades, they inhabit wet
conifer and mixed forests from sea level up to at least 3,500 feet
elevation, favoring sites where Douglas-fir and western red
cedar are dominant. They tend to be tree-top feeders and not as
inclined to visit backyard feeders. Their high-pitched, thin *tsee,
tsee, tsee, tsee* and thin, nasal *see soo* calls sound more like a
Golden-crowned Kinglet than a chickadee.

Adult. Smaller than
other chickadees. Cap
and throat patch dark
chocolate-brown, not
black. Back and flanks
rich chestnut brown.

Oak Titmouse

Baeolophus ridgwayi

L 6 | **WS** 16

The Oak Titmouse and the virtually identical Juniper Titmouse are both found in Oregon. While Junipers Titmice barely reach the state in extreme southern Lake County and perhaps southeastern Klamath County, Oak Titmice are commonly found in the central Rogue Valley, predominantly in areas with oaks and brushy understory. They are uncommon residents of oak and juniper woodlands in western and southern Klamath County. Vocalizations include an even-pitched staccato trill suggestive of a Bewick's Wren, a musical *thoo-wheet, thoo-wheet*, and nasal chatter and scolding notes.

Adult. Drab brownish-gray chickadee-sized bird with a distinct triangular crest. Stubby dark bill.

Bushtit

Psaltriparus minimus

L 3 | **WS** 6.25"

Except during the breeding season, Bushtits are highly gregarious birds, moving about in flocks of twenty to forty like a group of five-year-olds chasing a soccer ball. West of the Cascades, in the Klamath Basin, and along the Columbia River east to at least The Dalles, this species has a brown cap; farther east and away from the Columbia, only gray-crowned birds are found. Males have dark eyes and females have light eyes. Bushtits construct elaborate sock-like nests that seem large enough to host a small colony of birds their size; camouflaged with lichen and moss, the nest is hung inside low-hanging boughs of cedars and Douglas-firs. Vocalizations consist mostly of constant high-pitched twittering.

Adult male (gray-headed). In the interior, uniform gray without brown on the crown.

Adult female (brown-headed). Adult females have light eyes, while adult males and young birds of both sexes have dark eyes. Western birds have brown crowns.

Red-breasted Nuthatch

Sitta canadensis

L 7-8 | **WS** 7-8"

This bird spends much of its life upside down, creeping along branches and tree trunks poking around in the bark for food. Red-breasted Nuthatches also frequent visit backyard feeders, particularly those featuring suet. They are widespread residents all across Oregon, essentially anywhere there are conifers. They are generally absent from unforested parts of southeastern Oregon, but even there they pass through as spring and fall migrants. Red-breasted Nuthatches are semi-nomadic, moving about in response to food availability; year-to-year abundance at a site varies with the quality of the local cone crop. Cavity nesters, they usually excavate their own nest cavity, but sometimes use old woodpecker holes. Typical call is an incessant nasal *yank, yank, yank*.

Adult male. Black and white crown stripes. Rich reddish-brown below. Cold blue-gray back and wings. Female similar, with blue-gray crown stripes.

White-breasted Nuthatch

Sitta carolinensis

L 5–5.5 | **WS** 8–10.5"

Oregon's largest nuthatch has an affinity for dry, semi-open woodlands. It is absent from the coast and mostly treeless areas east of the Cascades, including the Columbia Plateau and southeastern Oregon, though migrants occasionally pass through those areas. West of the Cascades, White-breasted Nuthatches are generally found in oaks and, to a lesser extent, cottonwood forests along major rivers. East of the Cascades and away from the oak woodlands in Klamath and Wasco Counties, they are almost exclusively found in ponderosa pines. They do not occur up in the true firs and spruces. They are not as nomadic or as migratory as Red-breasted Nuthatches. They are cavity nesters, excavating their own holes or using old woodpecker cavities. Western Oregon birds give a *tooey, tooey, tooey*, interior birds give a more nasal *wha, wha, wha*.

Adult male. Cold blue-gray upper parts. Black crown and nape. Underparts almost entirely white, with a patch of rusty-brown on vent. Female has blue-gray crown.

Pygmy Nuthatch

Sitta pygmaea

L 3.5–4.25 | **WS** 8"

This small species has the most limited distribution of Oregon's nuthatches. Strictly a pine forest obligate, rarely wandering far from the nearest ponderosa pine, it is somewhat common along the drier eastern slopes of the Cascades and in the Warner, Ochoco, Blue, and Wallowa Mountains. Pygmy Nuthatches have occasionally strayed west into the Rogue Valley. The typical call is a sharp, high-pitched piping *peep, peep, peep*.

Adult. Smaller than other nuthatches, with brownish crown and cold blue-gray upper parts.

Brown Creeper

Certhia americana

L 5" | **WS** 8"

Brown Creepers work their way up the trunk of a tree head first, using their stiff tail feathers for support. A cryptic plumage pattern resembling tree bark makes them hard to spot. They are resident breeders throughout Oregon's woodlands. While generally found in conifers, they can also be quite abundant in pure stands of bottomland cottonwoods. The nests are concealed behind large sections of loose bark. Song is a high, thin series of notes that start high, descend in pitch in the middle, then end with ascending notes.

Adult. No other Oregon bird is quite like this cryptic brown sparrow-sized bird. It is always seen clinging vertically to the bark of a tree.

Rock Wren
Salpinctes obsoletus

L 4.75" | **WS** 9"

Found on rimrocks and dry rocky slopes throughout central and eastern Oregon and in the foothills of the Rogue Valley, this drab, tan wren is about 5 percent looks and 95 percent personality. Rock Wrens are frenetic and always on the move. When not bouncing from rock to rock and in and out of sight, they bob up and down constantly. About the time you are certain that you've lost track of a Rock Wren, there it is in plain view twenty feet away. Most Rock Wrens migrate out of the state to winter, but occasionally take a wrong turn and stray to atypical haunts such as a rock quarry in the Coast Range, a boulder in a Portland park, a jetty at the coast, or the face of a dam in the western Cascades. Their many vocalizations include energetic trills and buzzes.

Adult. Large tan wren with long, slightly downcurved bill. Doesn't cock its tail like other wrens.

Canyon Wren
Catherpes mexicanus

L 4.25–6" | **WS** 7.5"

These beautiful rusty-brown wrens are more often heard than seen. Inhabitants of towering rimrocks and steep river canyon walls, they too often are reluctant to venture down from their perches high on the cliffs. Canyon Wrens are uncommon to common breeders east of the Cascades anywhere there are tall basalt rimrocks and steep rocky canyons. A few overwinter, but most leave the state from October through March. Roaring Springs Ranch south of Frenglen, Harney County, and the volcanic neck at Fort Rock in northern Lake County are reliable places to see this charming bird. The cascading whistled song is protracted and loud; it gradually decelerates as if it were bouncing down the canyon wall towards you.

Adult. Medium-sized reddish-brown wren. Gleaming white breast. Bright rusty tail isn't held cocked.

House Wren

Troglodytes aedon

L 5" | **WS** 6"

This species is an uncommon to common breeder statewide except along the outer coast and in unwooded parts of Oregon. House Wrens are habitat generalists, taking advantage of woodland openings with brushy cover at almost any elevation and in all types of forest. Mid-elevation clearcuts, overgrown foothill pastures, and streamside brush are all places to expect House Wrens. They arrive in April and rarely linger in the state later than mid-October. Cavity nesters, they will occupy small nest boxes. Song is an energetic series of four or five trilled phrases on different pitches and at different speeds.

Adult. Smallish, plain brown wren with barred wings and tail. Tail frequently cocked. Upperparts medium earth-brown, underparts tan, paler and grayer on breast and throat.

Pacific Wren

Troglodytes pacificus

L 3-4.75" | **WS** 5-6"

If there were an award for sound per pound, this remarkable songster would surely win it. Pacific Wrens are tiny birds that rarely venture more than a few feet off the ground or leave the dark recesses of moist, heavily-shaded Pacific Northwest forests. They are common but reclusive residents of fern-covered, mossy slopes throughout western Oregon. They also inhabit wetter montane environs in the northeast corner of the state. The rollicking song of the Pacific Wren is impossible to ignore, nearly ten seconds of non-stop trills and chattering notes that constantly change pitch and speed.

Adult. Tiny chocolate-brown wren. Stubby cocked tail. Dark barring on belly and wings and tail. Always close to the ground.

Marsh Wren

Cistothorus palustris

L 5" | **WS** 6"

Marsh Wrens are present and usually abundant breeders in all of the state's major wetland complexes, where they weave their large nests into cattails, sedges, and other long-stemmed vegetation They often build multiple nests before laying eggs in one. As the nesting season cranks up, their scratch chattering scratchy songs seem to come from every direction. They are uncommon to common wintering birds at many of the breeding sites, especially on the more temperate westside; seasonally flooded swales and modest patches of sedge and reed-canary grass that dry up over the spring and summer provide ideal winter habitat. Boggy alder swamps with grassy understory in coastal dunes are great places to find a wintering Marsh Wren.

Adult. Warm reddish-brown above, buffy below with whiter throat. White and black streaking on upper back. Tail often cocked over back.

Bewick's Wren

Thyromanes bewickii

L 5" | **WS** 7"

Widely distributed and common residents of western Oregon lowlands, Bewick's Wrens are largely absent from eastern Oregon away from the Columbia River and the lowlands of southwest Klamath County. They are common in yards along the coast and in the interior westside valleys, and are also expected in brushy tangles, hedgerows, and blackberry mounds. Bewick's Wrens are unable to survive prolonged periods of sub-freezing temperatures and frozen ground. Songs, highly variable and often similar to those of Song Sparrows, usually start with two to four buzzy introductory notes, followed by a more musical, throaty trill. Call notes are usually raspy and scolding.

Adult. Medium-sized wren. Long tail usually cocked. Earth-brown to reddish-brown on crown, back, and wings. Gray below, paler and whiter towards throat. Most clearly defined white eyebrow of any Oregon wren.

Blue-gray Gnatcatcher

Polioptila caerulea

L 4.5" | **WS** 6"

This species has a very patchy distribution in Oregon, and shows strong preferences for just a few plant species. In the central Rogue Valley, Blue-gray Gnatcatchers are found only in and around wedgeleaf ceanothus, a tall tree-like bush with a dense canopy. East of the Cascades, there are scattered pockets of nesting gnatcatchers in mountain mahogany in Lake County, with occasional reports of breeding season birds in Klamath County and in western juniper in Crook and Harney Counties. The thin, wheezy calls are unlike those of any other Oregon bird.

Adult. Tiny, slender songbird with long skinny tail. Grayish-blue upperparts. Crisp white eye ring. White underparts. Long, narrow tail with white outer feathers, frequently twitched side to side.

American Dipper

Cinclus mexicanus

L 5.5-8" | **WS** 11.5"

The classic bird of fast-moving western streams, the American Dipper nests across most of Oregon where there are rock-strewn creeks and rivers, commonly in the Coast Range, Cascades, Siskiyou, Warner, Ochoco, and Blue and Wallowa Mountains. Nests, often built on the undersides of a bridge are large mossy structures about the size of bowling ball with an entrance in the side. Dippers perch on rocks, bobbing up and down on their sturdy pinkish legs. White excrement on midstream rocks is a clear sign that dippers are around. Song is a mockingbird-like series of double-noted buzzes and chirps. Call a high-pitched, sharp *zeet*.

Adult. Plump, upright, entirely dark gray. Looks like an over-sized wren. Dull pinkish legs.

Golden-crowned Kinglet

Regulus satrapa

L 4" | **WS** 7"

Kinglets are among the smallest North American songbirds.
Common breeders in mid- to higher-elevation conifer forests
statewide, Golden-crowned Kinglets are treetop birds,
spending much of their time buried in dense needles high in
the canopy, where they are difficult to see well. They are easiest
to find during the winter months, when they drop into the lower
elevations to join mixed feeding flocks with Chestnut-backed
Chickadees, Red-breasted Nuthatches, and other conifer-loving
birds. The very high-pitched song is inaudible
to many human ears.

Adult. Sexes similar. Tiny, plump, short-tailed
songbird. Striped black and white crown
with broad central panel of yellow-orange
in the center. Olive-green above, pale gray
below. Crisp white wing bars.

Ruby-crowned Kinglet

Regulus calendula

L 4.25″ | **WS** 7.5″

Ruby-crowned Kinglets are found in Oregon year-round, nesting from mid-May to August in sub-alpine fir forests. They winter at lower elevations, down to sea level, feeding in loose flocks with other small songbirds. Migratory movements can be quite impressive in April and September. Ruby-crowned King-lets are quite curious, responding readily to "pishing" sounds and owl imitations, and often come so close that binoculars aren't needed to get a good look. When agitated, males may raise the crown feathers to expose a usually hidden bright red patch. The wonderfully cheery song starts with a few high, thin notes, then accelerates into more musical twittering before ending with three or four clearly whistled *seecher, seecher, seecher* notes. Call is a harsh double-noted harsh scold, sometimes extended into a chatter.

Adult. Tiny, dull olive songbird with crisp eye ring and wing bars. Black patch between wing bars separates this species from similar Hutton's Vireo.

Wrentit

Chamaea fasciata

L 5.5-6" | **WS** 7"

Wrentits are secretive and generally sedentary, only occasionally popping out onto an open perch in the dense brushy vegetation and tangles they inhabit; they rarely fly. They are found along the full length of the coast, usually in dense patches of salal or boggy alder thickets; paler birds are found in the Rogue, Umpqua, and southern Willamette Valleys. They are also found upslope to 4000 feet on the west slope of the Cascades; their montane range extends north to at least Lane County. Song is an accelerating "bouncing ball" trill of clearly whistled notes. Calls have a rough, growling quality.

Adult. Sparrow-sized, with long cocked tail. Mostly dark chocolate-brown. Dark gray-brown head. Slightly paler and subtly streaked below.

Western Bluebird

Sialia mexicana

L 6.5-7.5" | **WS** 12.5"

After years of population declines caused by pesticides, habitat loss, and competition with non-native House Sparrows and European Starlings, the charming and stunningly beautiful Western Bluebird is recovering, thanks to habitat restoration and specially designed nest boxes. Western Bluebirds breed in valley foothills throughout Oregon, except in the arid southeastern corner. They inhabit oak savanna, semi-open woodlands, and grassy open slopes where nesting cavities are available. They are also found in brushy mid-elevation clearcuts. Song is a simple, stuttering series of whistled *kew* notes.

Adult male. Smaller than a robin. Deep sky-blue above. Rusty-brown upper back, rich rust-colored breast and flanks. White belly and undertail. Female similar to male, but less colorful, with blue-gray head and back.

Juvenile. Heavily streaked and spotted above and below. Gray head, brown back. Gray and brown beneath. Sky-blue wings and tail.

Mountain Bluebird
Sialia currucoides

L 6.5–8.0" | **WS** 13.5"

Far more migratory than Western Bluebirds, Mountain Bluebirds in April and May can seem to be perched on every third
section of the utility wires that line the highway from Bend to
Burns. Mountain Bluebirds nest almost exclusively east of the
Cascades crest, in habitats including high-elevation montane
meadows, semi-open pine and fir forests, burned stands of
timber, and even the wide-open sagebrush steppe. They are
cavity nesters, competing with Tree Swallows for abandoned
woodpecker holes in snags; because their typical haunts are
devoid of House Sparrows and European Starlings, they have
thus far not been subject to the population declines affecting
Western Bluebirds. The song is similar to the Western Bluebird's
but loweer-pitched, a more chortling series of *tew* notes somewhat similar to the calls of the Purple Martin.

Adult male. Stunning
and unmistakable.
Entirely rich sky-blue.

Adult female. Longer-winged
and with colder gray plumage
than female Western Bluebird.
Azure-blue in wings and tail.

Townsend's Solitaire

Myadestes townsendi

L 8" | **WS** 13"

Graceful and slender, the widespread Townsend's Solitaire breeds commonly throughout the mountains and juniper forests of central and eastern Oregon. This subtly colored thrush prefers drier, semi-open habitats such as forest openings and burned areas. In the Cascades, it is common on the eastern slopes but spotty in distribution on the western slopes; it is found sparingly in the Coast Range, predominantly in clearcuts at elevations above 2,000 feet. Not all solitaires leave for the winter; those that remain are almost always found around western junipers, feeding on waxy berries. Somewhat floppy wingbeats and light flight style are distinctive. The Townsend's Solitaire is a treetop singer, with a long-winded series of warbles that rise and fall in pitch. Call is a ringing, bell-like note, often repeated for minutes at a time.

Adult. Long-tailed and sleek robin-sized bird. Entirely gray. Bold white eye ring. Buffy patch at the base of the primaries. White outer tail feathers. Short dark bill. Juvenile is heavily mottled and spotted above and beneath.

Swainson's Thrush

Catharus ustulatus

L 7" | **WS** 12"

A denizen of moist forests, the Swainson's Thrush is one of western Oregon's most abundant breeding birds. The true density of the populations of this reclusive species in the Coast Range and valley foothills comes clear once you have learned its song and varied call notes. Swainson's Thrushes in the Cascades and western Oregon are warmer brown above, while more olive-backed birds nest in the Ochoco, Blue, and Wallowa Mountains. Completely absent from Oregon during winter, Swainson's Thrushes rarely arrive before the second week of May and typically depart by early October. During both spring and fall migrations, their rising *swee* or *weep* flight calls can be heard overhead, particularly on nights with low, dense cloud cover; on the outer coast, sometimes twenty calls a minutes can be heard, often peaking just before dawn. Distinctive fluting song spirals upwards in pitch. Most common call of perched birds is a liquid *whit*.

Adult Russet-backed. Western Oregon birds such as this one are rich, warm rusty-brown above, while interior mountain breeders are colder, darker olive-brown. Broad buffy eye ring Reddish-brown to olive-brown spotting on buffy breast.

Hermit Thrush

Catharus guttatus

L 6.75" | **WS** 11.5"

Hermit Thrushes breed at higher elevations in nearly all of Oregon's mountain ranges. They are sparse to rare breeders in the northern Coast Range. Above about 3,000 feet in the Cascades, and in drier forests with less dense understory, they replace Swainson's Thrushes as the expected breeding species. Smaller, darker Hermit Thrushes from Alaska winter uncommonly in the lowlands of western Oregon and sparsely east of the Cascades; this is the only brown-backed, spot-breasted thrush found in Oregon in winter. The fluting song starts with a single introductory note, then spirals downward in pitch. Call note is a soft *chup*.

Breeding adult. Contrasting rust-brown tail, often cocked. Gray-brown upperparts, whitish below, with large, well-scattered nearly black spots that extend onto belly. Crisp whitish eye ring. Wintering birds are smaller, dark earth-brown above.

American Robin

Turdus migratorius

L 10" | **WS** 14"

Instantly recognizable, for many the American Robin is like part of the family. We awake to a chorus of their songs, watch them pull worms from our lawns and gardens, get excited when we find a nest in our yard, and get even more excited when we see the first heavily spotted fledglings out the back window. Robins are abundant across much of Oregon throughout the year, though individual birds are highly migratory: The extent to which our wintering birds leave and are replaced during summer by birds that wintered farther south is poorly known. Song is a throaty series of phrases, *cheerily, cheer up, cheer up, cheerily, cheer up*. Calls include a *tuck, tuck* and a sharp *yeep* alarm note.

Adult male. Head darker than the rest of the gray upperparts. Broken white eye ring. Dark rusty-orange underparts. Undertail white with slate-gray streaks. Bill mostly orangish-yellow with dark tip.

Adult female. Like male, but paler head does not contrast with back. Underparts paler, with white often extending from undertail onto belly.

Juvenile. Just out of the nest smaller and shorter-tailed than adult. Upperparts gray-brown with white spotting. Heavily spotted breast and belly. Gradually acquires adult-like appearance by late summer or early fall.

Varied Thrush

Ixoreus naevius

L 8-10" | **WS** 13-15"

This distinctive thrush has a narrow distribution along the
Pacific Coast from Alaska to California. Varied Thrushes are
common breeders in the Coast Range and along the western
slope of the Cascades, less common in more easterly ranges.
They occupy wet dense forests, spending most of their time at
higher elevations. One of the best ways to see this bird is to
drive quiet mountain roads early in the morning, when they can
sometimes be seen by the dozens. Although migratory, Varied
Thrushes are found in Oregon year-round. When snow hits
the mid-elevation slopes where they winter, they frequently
descend into the lowlands, often becoming quite numerous
around filbert orchards and apple trees with downed or rotting
fruit. Song is a unique vibrating metallic trill, simultaneously
humming and whistling. Call is a soft, throaty *chuck*.

Adult male. Robin-like in size and general appearance, but shorter-tailed. Upperparts
dusky grayish-blue. Orangish-buff eyebrow, no eye ring. Rusty-orange underparts with
broad, dark dusky-blue breast band. Buffy-orange wing bars and patches in wings. Mostly
dark bill. Female like male, but paler overall. Belly and lower flanks more scaly in
appearance.

Gray Catbird

Dumetella carolinensis

L 8.5" | **WS** 11"

Gray Catbirds are uncommon streamside breeders in Union, Wallowa, Umatilla, and perhaps Baker Counties. There have also been regular reports of catbirds summering in Deschutes and Klamath Counties, suggesting a range expansion along the east slope of the Cascades. Only a few catbirds pass through the Harney County migrant sites each spring, and they are rare strays west of the Cascades. Though they are roughly robin-sized, catbirds are easily overlooked unless you recognize their vocalizations. They skulk in dense willow tangles making lots of noise, but remaining mostly out of sight. Catbirds are mimics, creating a song out of a mix of phrases appropriated from other species. A cat-like *mew* is the one sound truly their own.

Adult. Entirely slate-gray with black cap. Eye and bill dark.

Sage Thrasher

Oreoscoptes montanus

L 7.75–9" | **WS** 12.5"

The smallest thrasher on the North American continent, this is the only species that occurs regularly in Oregon, where it is one of the two or three most abundant breeding birds in the sagebrush landscapes of southeastern Oregon. Sage Thrashers also breed in uncultivated, treeless habitats on the Columbia Plateau where sage and other scrubby shrub species are the dominant vegetation. The territorial display includes an arcing, banking flight. Sage Thrashers sing day and night during the breeding season, and in the high desert are likely to be the first bird heard in the morning and the last heard at night . Song is a rambling series of warbled phrases that can go on for minutes at a time.

Adult. Grayish sandy-brown above. Buffy below with dark, heavy streaks. Yellow eye. Bill short and straight.

Northern Mockingbird

Mimus polyglottos

L 10" | **WS** 14"

Well known for the ability to mimic the songs and calls of other birds, Northern Mockingbird pairs occasionally nest in southeastern Oregon, but have not become established there. Since first nesting in the Rogue Valley in 1993, this species has become a very uncommon permanent resident around Medford, Central Point, and White City. Mockingbirds occasionally winter farther north along the coast and in the Willamette Valley, sometimes returning to the same site for several consecutive winters.

Adult. Long-tailed and slender. Light gray above, paler pearl-gray below. White wing bars. Conspicuous white wing patches and white outer tail feathers in flight.

European Starling

Sturnus vulgaris

L 8.5" | **WS** 14"

The non-native European Starling was first introduced to Oregon in the late nineteenth century, but not until the 1940s did birds moving west from established eastern populations establish a permanent presence in the state. Starlings are now abundant in most parts of Oregon, typically around human habitation and in disturbed landscapes, thriving as much in urban and suburban areas as in woodland openings and farm-land. They are scarce away from towns in southeastern Oregon and are not found in heavily forested areas. Often competing with native cavity-nesters, they build nests in natural cavi-ties, nest boxes, and vents and crevices in buildings. They are accomplished mimics, some individuals imitating a dozen or more different species. They seem particular fond of imitating the Western Wood-Pewee, often starting well before that species arrives in spring.

Adult. Plump and short-tailed compared to blackbirds. All-dark plumage with iridescent greens and purples. Small buffy spots on most feathers. Bright yellow bill.

Juvenile. Uniformly dark dirt-brown. Dark bill.

House Sparrow
Passer domesticus

L 6" | **WS** 10"

This Old World species, not closely related to the New World birds known as sparrows, arrived in Oregon near the end of the nineteenth century and quickly became established around towns and farms statewide. Though abundant where present, House Sparrows are rarely found away from human habitation. These aggressive cavity-nesters are known to remove or destroy the eggs of bluebirds, wrens, and other native birds in their effort to take over a nest box. They also nest in vents and crevices in houses, barns, and commercial buildings. Prolific breeders, they often rear more than one brood a year. Call is a loud *cheep* or *chirrup*.

Adult male. Plump and sparrow-like. Thick triangular black bill. Upperparts mostly rich chestnut. Single broad white wing bar. Crown pale gray. Variable amount of black on throat and upper breast, otherwise dingy gray beneath.

Adult female. Nondescript, sandy-brown and sparrow-like. Head proportionally large and flat-crowned. Streaked back. Pale buffy supercilium.

Cedar Waxwing

Bombycilla cedrorum

L 7" | **WS** 12"

The Cedar Waxwing looks as if it had come from an artist's palette, with the last step being a dip of the tail in a can of yellow paint. Present across Oregon year-round, this species is an uncommon to common nester in riparian habitats and sometimes an abundant fall migrant. Their winter distribution is highly food-dependent. Waxwings almost exclusively eat hard waxy berries such as those found on western juniper, mountain ash, and pyracantha. When they find a tree or bush to their liking, they will return day after day until it is picked clean. The Cedar Waxwing's vocalization is an extremely fast, high-pitched metallic trill inaudible to some human ears.

Adult. Slightly smaller than a starling. Buffy gray-brown and crested. Black mask through eye. Lower belly and undertail pale yellow. Broad yellow tip on tail. Waxy red tips on secondaries.

Juvenile. Crest abbreviated or absent. Duller and dingier than adult, with heavy streaking below. Yellow-tipped tail.

Bohemian Waxwing

Bombycilla garrulus

L 6-8" | **WS** 13"

The larger of North America's two waxwing species is strictly a winter bird in Oregon. Large flocks can typically be found in northeast Oregon from December to March, but Bohemian Waxwings are rare at other seasons and elsewhere in the state, occasionally turning up as single individuals in flocks of Cedar Waxwings. Most winter sightings of these sleek, crested birds come from Umatilla, Union, and Wallowa Counties, normally in and around towns where ornamental and native trees with waxy berries provide a stable source of food.

Adult. Larger than Cedar Waxwing. Plumage mostly gray. Rust-colored face, black eye mask and chin. Undertail rich rusty-brown. Tail broadly tipped yellow. White, red, and yellow wing pattern more colorful than Cedar Waxwing's.

American Pipit
Anthus rubescens

L 6.5" | **WS** 10.5"

American Pipits are uncommon nesters in alpine areas of several of the state's highest peaks, but are not found below timberline during the breeding season. They are much more frequently encountered in migration and winter. The epicenter of their winter abundance is the southern Willamette Valley. Flocks of up to 200 birds frequent the expansive muddy grass fields and sheep pastures in Linn and northern Lane Counties November–March. They are locally uncommon during winter along the coast and in the lowlands of western Oregon's inland valleys. In spring and, especially, fall migration, large flocks can be found move through eastern Oregon and along the outer coast. Pipits habitually wag their tails up and down while perched or feeding. Call is a high-pitched, sometimes squeaky and slurred *peep-it*.

Winter Adult. Slender, sparrow-sized; rather long tail constantly wagged. Olive-brown and barely streaked above. Buffy below, with highly variable amounts of olive-brown streaking on upper breast and flanks. Ears framed by pale creamy white eye brow and jaw stripe. Breeding adults are rarely seen in Oregon. They have plain pale gray upper parts. Underparts peachy-pinkish with variable amounts of breast streaking.

Evening Grosbeak

Coccothraustes vespertinus

L 7" | **WS** 12-14"

Loud, gregarious and a bit comical looking, Evening Grosbeaks are uncommon to common breeders in mid- to high-elevation conifer forests in all of Oregon's major mountain ranges. Like most conifer seed-eating finches, Evening Grosbeaks are unpredictable winter nomads; in years when they are abundant, they are a backyard feeder favorite, unless you are paying for the seed. They are most abundant and easiest to see during spring migration, when they invade the lowlands to feast on the buds of deciduous trees, especially maples and elms. ATt peak migration time in the Willamette Valley, between the third week of April and mid-May, it can be hard to walk outside in Eugene or Corvallis without hearing the calls of Evening Grosbeaks feeding or flying overhead. The calls are mix of loud, piercing *keers* and burry chattering *churrrps*.

Adult male. Large yellow and black finch with a huge, grayish olive conical bill. Dusky brown head with bright yellow eyebrow. Dirty yellow breast with brighter yellow belly and wing coverts. Wings black with large white patch. Black tail.

Adult female. Females are mostly gray, darker above and on head. Massive bill varies in color from pale greenish to yellowish. Yellow on collar and nape. Black wings with smaller white patch than male.

Gray-crowned Rosy-Finch
Leucosticte tephrocotis

L 5.5–8.25" | **WS** 13"

Only mountain climbers and alpine hikers are likely to see this species during the breeding season, when it nests in crevices of rocky outcrops above timberline. Most rosy-finches remain at higher elevations in the winter, but some move to lower elevations. A small flock winters each year near the summit of Mary's Peak southwest of Corvallis, the only place in the Coast Range where they regularly occur. They are also found in the foothill valleys of the Blue and Wallowa Mountains during winter. Golf Course Road, north of Enterprise in Wallowa County, is a particular reliable and accessible place to see this bird; flocks of hundreds often feed right along the road. At dusk they go to roost in old wooden barns and dilapidated outbuildings. Call is a buzzy, sometimes slurred *chew*.

Adult male. Sparrow-sized; short-legged and plump. Mostly rich chocolate-brown, with extensive pink in wing and on lower belly and undertail. Black forehead and chin. Amount of gray on head varies.

Adult female. Female similar, but with less pink on wings and underparts. Gray on head generally duller.

Black Rosy-Finch
Leucosticte atrata

L 5.5-6.25" | **WS** 13"

Black Rosy-Finches breed in Oregon only around rocky
outcrops and snowfields near the summit of Steens Mountain,
and even there they are by no means abundant. Snow covers
this mountaintop late into the year, and the road to the summit
rarely opens before mid-July. In winter, they are rare in the
Alvord Desert in the basin just east of the mountain, and there
are a handful of winter records from Wallowa County, where
Blacks have been found in large flocks of Gray-crowned Rosy-
Finches. Call is a buzzy *chew*.

Adult male. Plump, sparrow-sized. Mostly
dark dusky-brown. Broad pink panel in wing,
pink on lower belly and undertail. Gray
through eye wraps across nape. Female
almost all dark.

House Finch

Haemorhous mexicanus

L 5" | **WS** 9"

This wide-ranging resident is found throughout the state almost anywhere there is human habitation. House Finches frequent backyard sunflower feeders, and are common in urban, suburban, and other disturbed habitats where the human footprint is evident. They often build their nests on houses, sometimes in front door wreaths or hanging planters. In some males, the red in the plumage is replaced by paler orange or, more rarely, yellow. Song is an energetic but disorganized warble that typically ends with a hard upslurred note. Call is a slightly nasal and up-slurred *chew-ep*.

Adult male (above). Sparrow-sized. Red on forehead and breast. Brown crown with red sides. Broad, blurry streaks on belly and undertail. Back and tail pale sandy brown. Upper ridge of bill is slightly curved. Female (right). Entirely sand-brown above. Minimal pattern on head. Weak wing bars. Underparts creamy whitish and heavily streaked. Streaks are broad and blurry.

Purple Finch

Haemorhous purpureus

L 6" | **WS** 10"

More migratory than the similar House Finch, Purple Finches are forest and woodland birds that nest mostly away from human habitation. Common breeders in the mountains and foothills from the Cascades crest westward, they are less common nesters along the east slope of Cascades; there are only a few pockets of breeders in the Ochoco and Blue Mountains, where they are otherwise replaced by Cassin's Finches. Purple Finches inhabit a variety of forest types, almost always with some conifers in the mix. Most leave the state in winter, with a few remaining in the westside lowlands and along the coast. The song, a fast rising warble sometimes transcribed as *meteor, meteor, meteor*, is almost always offered from the top of a conifer. Occasionally gives a series of widely spaced two-note chortles that suggest a vireo song. Call note is a dry, flat *pik*.

Adult male. Stockier and shorter-tailed than House Finch. Crown entirely red, with some red or rosy on back. Breast more pinkish. Unstreaked lower belly and undertail. Upper ridge of bill slightly curved.

Adult female. Compared to House Finch, darker brown above, often with a greenish cast. Strong head pattern with pale supercilium and jaw stripe framing dark cheek patch. Underparts show more contrast, with darker, slightly crisper streaking. Unstreaked undertail.

Cassin's Finch
Haemorhous cassinii

L 6.25" | **WS** 10–10.75"

This species essentially replaces the Purple Finch east of the Cascades as the common red finch of forest habitats. Cassin's Finches are most abundant in drier pine and pine–juniper forests, but far less common in damper fir-spruce stands. They are common breeders along the east slope of the Cascades and in the Ochoco and Blue Mountains, less common in the Wallowas. Most migrate out of upslope breeding areas for the winter. Cassin's Finches are accomplished mimics, often inserting snippets of other species' vocalizations into their songs. Song is a complicated fast warble, with more distinct phrases than the song of a Purple Finch. Call is a two-noted *cha-lip*, given at different pitches with long pauses in between; pattern is suggestive of a vireo song.

Adult male. Similar to male Purple Finch, but noticeably redder crown contrasts with the rest of the more pinkish head and breast. Underparts unstreaked. Bill longer and more pointed, with very straight ridge.

Adult female. Similar to female Purple Finch, but paler and sandier overall. Streaking on underparts narrower and crisper than in female House and Purple finches. Undertail streaked. Very pointed bill with straight upper ridge.

Pine Siskin

Spinus pinus

L 5" | **WS** 7–9"

Pine Siskins are found in coniferous and mixed forests; in Oregon, their name notwithstanding, they tend to be least abundant in stands dominated by pine. They breed in all of Oregon's major mountain ranges and associated foothills, their abundance varying from year to year with cone crops. Winter numbers are remarkably changeable. In some years, clouds of siskins appear in red alders, spruces, and firs along the coast and in the Coast Range or in ornamental birches in cities and towns all across Oregon. In other years they may go almost unrecorded. Song is a mix of burry and nasal chattered notes. Call is a rising buzzy *zeee*.

Adult male. Small, slender, gray-brown finch. Heavily marked with crisp dark streaking above and below. Varying amount of yellow or greenish yellow in wing and tail. Bill tiny and sharply pointed.

Adult female/ immature. Female and immature generally lack yellow. Pale whitish wing bars. Smaller and more crisply streaked than similar female House Finch, with much smaller, more sharply pointed bill.

Red Crossbill

Loxia curvirostra

L 7" | **WS** 10"

Crossbills are conifer obligates, feeding almost exclusively on seeds extracted from pine, fir, and spruce cones that they pry open with their distinctive crossed beaks. They breed in all of Oregon's major mountain ranges, but year-to-year abundance varies with the quality of the cone crop. Crossbills are highly nomadic in winter, when they can be wholly absent from an area or remarkably abundant, depending on food supply. Calls are single- or double-noted, ranging from a hollow, woody *kip-kip* or *toop* to higher-pitched *jip-jip* or *jeep*.

Adult male. Large, plump finch; varies from deep red to paler, more orangish red. Brownish wing with no wing bars. Heavy bill with crossed tip.

Adult female. Varies from dull olive-yellow to more orangish or rich greenish yellow. May have some dusky streaking below.

Lesser Goldfinch
Spinus psaltria

L ?" | **WS** 7.75"

Smaller and more compact than the American Goldfinch, the Lesser Goldfinch is widespread and common throughout the lowland valleys of western Oregon. East of the Cascades, this species' distribution is more patchy and restricted to drier lowlands. Nesting has been documented as far east as the state's eastern border in Malheur County. They are remarkable mimics. The songs are mostly grating chatter, with phrases of other species' songs mixed in. Common calls are a protracted *teeer* and a dry chattering *chup, chup, chup*.

Adult male. Tiny finch with black cap, olive-green back, and bright lemon-yellow underparts. Dark, sometimes black wings. Conspicuous white wing patches in flight.

Female/immature. Female and immature vary from fairly bright greenish yellow to extremely dull grayish olive. Inconspicuous wing bars. Small conical bill.

American Goldfinch

Spinus tristis

L 4.5-5" | **WS** 7.5-9"

American Goldfinches are common to abundant breeders across most of Oregon, nesting primarily in riparian bottomlands and cottonwood forests. They are generally uncommon during winter, when flocks remain only in places with a stable food supply, such as backyard feeders. Song is an extended mix of buzzy chattering notes and sweeter, more musical warbled phrases. Commonly heard flight call a bubbling *potato chip*.

Breeding adult male. Breeding male bright lemon-yellow with black cap and pink bill. Black wings with bold white wing bar.

Breeding adult female. Breeding female similar to male, but lacks black cap and is paler yellow.

Winter Adult. Dull yellow on head (brighter in male). Blend of tawny pale brown and soft pearl-gray above and below. Blackish wings with two bold wing bars and pale buffy secondaries.

Immature. Pale buffy tan with minimal yellow on face. Black wings with two broad buffy wing bars.

Green-tailed Towhee

Pipilo chlorurus

L 7" | **WS** 10"

The breeding range of Green-tailed Towhees in Oregon falls beneath a line drawn from the northeastern corner of the state to Ashland. These richly colored sparrows summer in dry brushy openings and semi-open pine forests along the eastern slope of the Cascades from about Madras south. They are locally uncommon in the southern Blue Mountains, but are generally scarce or absent farther north. In Klamath, Lake, Harney, and Malheur Counties, they can be found in pine and juniper forests with dense chaparral-like understory. Inside the bowl at Fort Rock is a reliable place to see this bird. The song starts and ends with rough buzzy notes bracketing a sweeter whistled trill. Call is high-pitched, nasal *mew*.

Adult. Male and female similar. Distinctive rusty-red cap and white throat. Underparts otherwise medium-gray. Wings and tail bronzy-green.

Spotted Towhee
Pipilo maculatus

L 6.75–8.25" | **WS** 11"

A common denizen of shaded understory statewide, Spotted Towhees are regular visitors to backyard feeders during the winter months. They are short-distance migrants. The population that nests along the coast and in the Willamette Valley shows the least amount of white spotting above, while those that nest in southwestern Oregon and east of the Cascades are heavily spotted. They generally stay low in brushy tangles, but breeding males choose the tops of tall snags and trees for territorial singing. Feeding behavior includes vigorous scratching and kicking in leaf litter. Song is fast trilled *tow-heeeee* or *tow-tow-heeeee*. Call is a loud, harsh, catlike *mew*.

Male Coastal. White corners on tail. Rusty robin-colored flanks. White down center of breast and belly. Eye blood red. Conical black bill. Coastal and Willamette Valley breeders have only limited white spotting on scapulars and wing coverts. Female similar to male but head, back, and tail with brownish cast.

Male Interior. Breeders have heavy white spotting forming white lines on the wing and back.

California Towhee

Melozone crissalis

L 8.25-10" | **WS** 11.5"

Few species have a more limited Oregon range than the drab brown California Towhee, a chaparral specialist typically tied to extensive stands of ceanothus. This nearly robin-sized sparrow is resident in the Rogue Valley and locally rare near Klamath Falls. Single birds have occasionally resided for a time in central Douglas County, but California Towhees have never become firmly established there. Like other towhees, this species scratches the ground and leaf litter when looking for food. Song starts with a series of sweet clear notes, then accelerates to harsher grating notes at the end. Call is sharp metallic *chink* or *spink*.

Adult. Almost entirely dirt-brown, with rusty undertail coverts and some rusty feathering around the base of the bill.

Yellow-breasted Chat

Icteria virens

L 7.5" | **WS** 9.5"

Yellow-breasted Chats are noisy but secretive birds of dense streamside thickets and foothill brush fields. They are found most commonly east of the Cascades, along willow-lined canyons such as those found along the Deschutes, John Day, and Umatilla Rivers. They are also common along the Blitzen River in the southern part of Malheur N.W.R. They are generally less abundant west of the Cascades, but are present in the bottomlands of the Columbia and Willamette Rivers and along the Santiam, McKenzie, Umpqua, and Rogue Rivers. Chats are generally rare on the outer coast. Song is a diverse assortment of loud raspy caws, mews, and rattles, along with whistled phrases strung together in random order. Call is a harsh, nasal *skew*.

Adult. Towhee-sized, with thick tanager-like bill. Gleaming yellow throat and breast. Belly whitish. Dark gray head with broad white eye brow and eye ring. Back, wings, and tail are olive-brownish.

Chipping Sparrow

Spizella passerina

L 5.5" | **WS** 8.5"

One of Oregon's smallest sparrows, the Chipping Sparrow has a nearly statewide breeding distribution, but it is generally uncommon west of the Cascades as a nester. It breeds most abundantly in dry montane pine and fir forests, with the highest densities in lodgepole pine stands east of the crest of the Cascades and in the eastern mountain ranges. Chipping Sparrows are also numerous in mixed stands of western juniper and ponderosa pine with some underbrush. During fall migration, large flocks move through central and eastern Oregon. Chipping Sparrows winter sparingly in the state, most often around filbert and fruit orchards and berry patches in the westside lowlands. Young White-crowned Sparrows are occasionally misidentified as this species, but are much larger, with bright bills. Song is a flat, dry, insect-like trill. Call is a soft high-pitched *chip*.

Breeding adult. Small, slender sparrow with distinctive red crown and white eye brow. Upperparts pale earth-brown with darker streaks. Rump gray. Two crisp white wing bars. Dark eyeline extends in front of eye to bill. Underparts pale pearl-gray.

Non-Breeding adult/immature. Rusty-brown crown with poorly defined central stripe. Buffy eye brow contrasts with darker dusky-brown ear patch. Underparts dingier and buffer than breeding adult's.

Brewer's Sparrow

Spizella breweri

L 5-6" | **WS** 7.75"

As a dawn stop in breeding season between Bend and Burns will show, the drab little Brewer's Sparrow more than makes up for its understated appearance with a complex buzzing and trilling song that rings out over the sagebrush. It breeds abundantly in this habitat, which covers much of southeastern Oregon. Brewer's Sparrows are also found in semi-open pine and juniper woodlands with sage or similar understory. They are highly migratory, retreating to the desert southwest and Mexico to winter. They are a rare but annual visitor west of the Cascades.

Adult. Small brown streak-backed, pale-breasted sparrow. Minimal face pattern. Weak wing bars. Solid brown crown is finely streaked with black but has no pale central stripe. Pale lores. Mostly pink bill.

Vesper Sparrow

Pooecetes gramineus

L 5-6" | **WS** 9"

Still thriving in grassland and open country habitats east of the
Cascades, the western Oregon population of Vesper Sparrows is
quickly disappearing and already gone from much of its former
range in the Willamette, Umpqua and Rogue Valleys, where
oak savanna grasslands are being lost at an alarming rate to
housing developments, vineyards, orchards, and nurseries. On
the eastside, Vespers remain common to abundant breeders
in shorter patches of sage and remnant prairie habitats such
those at Zumwalt Prairie in Wallowa County. They also breed
at higher elevations on unforested ridges and peaks like Steens
and Hart Mountains. Song starts with two clearly-whistled
notes, then a buzzy note or two before short throaty trill. Call
note is sharp and high-pitched.

Adult. Medium-sized, long-tailed
sparrow with streaked breast.
Conspicuous eye ring, rusty
shoulder patch, and white outer
tail feathers separate this species
from similar sparrows.

Lark Sparrow

Chondestes grammacus

L 6-7" | **WS** 11"

Its strongly patterned head and broad, white-edged tail make the Lark Sparrow easy to identify. East of the Cascades, it is a widespread, uncommon to common breeder in open grassland and sagebrush habitats with patches of bare sandy soil. It is also found around the edges of plowed fields and other sites where human activities have created weedy patches or bare ground in otherwise unbroken grassland and sagebrush habitats. West of the Cascades, the breeding range of Lark Sparrow is limited to the Rogue Valley, where it is a locally uncommon nester. Song is a complicated jumble of short buzzes and trills at varied pitches. Call note is sharp and high-pitched.

Adult. Large sparrow with striking chestnut, black, and white head pattern. Plain-breasted, with black central spot. In flight, note distinctive black and white pattern on broad tail.

Black-throated Sparrow

Amphispiza bilineata

L 4.75-5.5"   **WS** 8.5"

In most years, these classic desert sparrows breed only in extreme southeastern Oregon. Fort Rock is the most northerly site where this species can be expected, but drought in the heart of the normal breeding range sometimes pushes Black-throated Sparrows even farther north. They are most abundant in the rain shadow of Steens Mountain and neighboring Pueblo Mountains. Inhabiting slopes with limited vegetation and scattered boulders, Black-throated Sparrows are generally easy to hear and see singing from the tops of large boulders just upslope from the road along the western edge of the Alford Desert north of Fields. A pair or two have also traditionally nested on the south-facing slope of Wright's Point between Burns and Malheur N.W.R. headquarters.

Adult. Sexes similar. Medium-sized sparrow with striking gray and white head pattern. Black throat extends to the central breast.

Sagebrush Sparrow

Artemisiospiza nevadensis

L 4.75-6" | **WS** 8.25"

On their Oregon breeding grounds, Sagebrush Sparrows are found only in large, dense patches of tall thriving sagebrush, often at the foot of rimrocks and other basalt formations that funnel additional rainwater to low-lying areas. It is a fool's errand to look for Sagebrush Sparrows in an undernourished parcel of widely-spaced stunted sage with lots of bare ground in between. Song is buzzy, rising and falling in pitch with a sing-song rhythm.

Adult. Sexes similar. Distinctive gray head and black jaw stripe frame the white throat. Underparts mostly white, with blackish central breast spot.

Savannah Sparrow

Passerculus sandwichensis

L 4.25–6.25" | **WS** 7.75–8.5"

Savannah Sparrows vary individually and geographically in
size, bill size, plumage tone, and amount of streaking. A yellow
wash through the lores and eye brow is seen in most. Savannah
Sparrows breed commonly in open grasslands, grassy dunes,
and cultivated grass crops throughout the state. In winter, they
are largely limited to the westside lowlands. They are readily
found in cultivated grains such as winter wheat and rye grass in
the southern Willamette Valley, and they also occur abundantly
in coastal dairy pastures, where large flocks of fall migrants
can be conspicuous. Song features a short burst of musical
introductory notes followed by an extended buzzy, insect-like
trill. Call is a high, thin *tseet*.

All ages. All ages similar. Small,
short-tailed sparrow with
streaked upperparts. White
below, with crisp dark streaking
on breast and upper belly;
central breast spot. Varying
amounts of yellow in lores and
supercilium. Flesh-pink legs.

Grasshopper Sparrow
Ammodramus savannarum

L 4.5" | **WS** 8.25"

Away from a few traditional sites, the year-to-year distribution of nesting Grasshopper Sparrows in Oregon is unpredictable. Changing land use often forces colonies to move. Preferred sites have grasses of mixed heights, with taller shrubs or long-stemmed grasses as singing perches. There are only a few long-term colonies on the westside; one on the westside of Fern Ridge Reservoir and another along Belts Road near Brownsville, Linn County, are easily accessible. On the eastside, Grasshopper Sparrows are most readily found on the Columbia Plateau in the northern tier counties between the Cascades and the Blue Mountains. The huge grassland along the westside of Bombing Range Road south of Boardman, Morrow County, has a sizable population. Grasshopper Sparrows can also be found at Zumwalt Prairie in Wallowa County. Song is an extremely high-pitched, insect-like buzz that can be difficult to hear.

Adult. Small, short-tailed, flat-headed sparrow with large bill. Unstreaked buffy underparts. Upperparts pale sandy brown with reddish brown streaks on back.

Fox Sparrow
Passerella iliaca

L 7" | **WS** 10"

Oregon is a crossroads for the extremely variable Fox Sparrow, where four more or less distinctive "flavors" meet. The "Sooty" Fox Sparrow is the expected wintering form in the western half of the state. "Red" Fox Sparrows are rare but annual winter strays to Oregon. The "Slate-colored" Fox Sparrow nests in the Blue and Wallowa Mountains, and migrants occasionally appear at Harney County oases. The "Thick-billed" Fox Sparrow nests commonly in the Siskiyou Mountains and throughout the Cascades north to near the Columbia River; it probably breeds in the mountains of southeastern Oregon as well.

Slate-colored Fox Sparrows are dark gray on the head and upper back, with contrastingly rusty brown wings and tail.

Thick-billed. Similar in plumage to Slate-coloreds, Thick-billed Fox Sparrows have a large triangular bill, quite deep at the base.

Sooty Fox Sparrows are solid dark chocolate brown above with little if any face pattern.

Red Fox Sparrows show strongly contrasting patterns of rusty-brown and gray. Gray rump contrasts with rusty tail.

Song Sparrow

Melospiza melodia

L 5-7" | **WS** 7-9"

Song Sparrows are resident and widely distributed breeders statewide, almost always near a reliable source of water. In the winter months, eastside birds retreat from higher elevations to lowland areas, often to streamside thickets. Birds resident in most of western Oregon are larger and darker than those found east of the. Typical song starts with two or three clear introductory notes followed by a trill. Call is a fairly loud *jeep*.

Coastal Adult. Song Sparrows along the coast and throughout the western lowlands are large, and darker reddish-brown above and grayer below than interior forms. Streaking beneath is reddish brown.

Interior Adult. Smaller interior birds are more earth-toned, streaked above and whiter on the underparts, with duskier streaks.

Lincoln's Sparrow

Melospiza lincolnii

L 6" | **WS** 8"

Lincoln's Sparrows breed in higher-elevation bogs in the spruce and fir forests in the Cascades and in the Siskiyou, Ochoco, Warner, Blue, and Wallowa Mountains. They are uncommon spring and fall migrants, with modest numbers overwintering west of the Cascades. More secretive than the closely related Song Sparrow, Lincoln's Sparrows are perhaps more inclined to be found in deep swales, wetlands, and other low-lying areas with standing water. Song, rarely heard away from the breeding grounds, is a mix of trilled and gurgled buzzy notes. Other vocalizations include a hard chip and a buzzy *zzzst*.

Adult. Smaller and more slender than Song Sparrow, with buffier face pattern. Fine, crisp streaking ends abruptly across the middle of the buff-washed breast.

White-throated Sparrow

Zonotrichia albicollis

L 7" | **WS** 9"

Once only rare winter visitors, White-throated Sparrows are now merely very uncommon wintering birds along the Pacific Coast. In Oregon, most appear west of the Cascades; they are still rare on the eastside in winter. Spring and fall migrants are increasingly regular both east and west of the Cascades. Adults show either a white or tan supercilium. Song is a musical series of clear whistled notes, *Old Sam Peabody, Peabody* or *Oh sweet Canada, Canada*. Call is a hard metallic *chink*.

Large, plump sparrow with broad black and white or tan head stripes. Well-defined white throat. Yellow above and in front of the eye. Immature duller, with less obvious throat patch.

Golden-crowned Sparrow

Zonotrichia atricapilla

L 6-7" | **WS** 10"

Golden-crowned Sparrows are present in Oregon from early
September through mid-May, typically in more densely
vegetated habitats than White-crowned Sparrows. Common
at backyard feeders, these colorful-headed birds offer a great
opportunity to monitor feather replacement in a wild bird as
the crown changes from dull gold and brown to striking black,
white, and yellow before the spring migration. The song is a
mournful whistle, *I am so sad*. Call is a loud, crisp whistled *seep*
that suggests the call of a phoebe.

Adult. Large, plump sparrow with
dingy earth-brown upperparts and
dirty brownish gray underparts.
Distinctive crown pattern with broad
black stripes separated by a broad
yellow stripe, white on the hind crown.

Immature. Similar to
adult, but lacks black
crown stripes. Entire
forecrown golden
yellowish.

White-crowned Sparrow

Zonotrichia leucophrys

L 6" | **WS** 10"

Found in open country and forest openings, White-crowned Sparrows breed in the Cascades and western Oregon, where they are generally sedentary, migrating only short distances if at all. Breeders in the higher mountains east of the Cascades winter in the southwestern U.S. and Mexico. Spring and fall see a few Canadian and Alaskan breeders moving through the state on their way to wintering grounds in the southwestern U.S.. The different populations vary subtly in face pattern and bill color, as do their buzzy whistled songs. Call is a moderately loud metallic *tsink*.

Adult Puget Sound. Black and white or whitish crown stripes, colorful bill, and gray to buffy-gray underparts easily distinguish this species from the superficially similar White-throated Sparrow.

Adult Mountain. The only dark-lored, pink-billed form of White-crowned Sparrow found in Oregon.

Immature. Head pattern similar to adult's, but tan and rusty rather than black and white. Underparts brownish buff.

Dark-eyed Junco

Junco hyemalis

L 6" | **WS** 9"

Well-known and widespread, Dark-eyed Juncos are common
to abundant year-round residents in most of Oregon. Their
seasonal movements here tend to be elevational between
wintering and breeding grounds. Most breeding occurs in
upslope conifer woodlands, but many remain to nest in the
lowlands not far from where they spent the winter months. The
brightly colored "Oregon" Dark-eyed Juncos breed statewide,
except in the mostly treeless southeastern corner of the state.
Plainer gray "Slate-colored" Dark-eyed Juncos from the north
and east move into Oregon in modest numbers in winter.

Adult male. "Oregon" Juncos have dark
heads and brown backs, with warm brownish
wash on flanks. Males are blacker on the
head, females grayer.

Adult male. "Slate-colored" entirely slate-gray to blackish above and white below, with no obvious brown on the back.

Juvenile. Fresh juveniles are heavily streaked, but the white outer tail feathers, shown by all ages and both sexes of juncos, reveal their identity.

Bobolink

Dolichonyx oryzivorus

L 7" | **WS** 12"

Smaller and more compact than a Red-winged Blackbird, this member of the blackbird family is a widespread semi-colonial breeder that is common east of the Rockies. West of the Rockies Bobolink distribution is patchy. Eastern Oregon lies at the far western edge of their breeding range, thus they are not always present in suitable habitat. Nesting areas are usually seasonally flooded pastures and wet valley meadows irrigated by spring runoff. There are numerous colonies in Wallowa, Baker, Grant and Harney counties, with isolated breeding outposts elsewhere. Bobolinks are rare fall strays to the outer coast. Displaying males circle low over their territory with shallow fluttering wingbeats all the while belting out a long bubbling stream of metallic and buzzy notes that are typically heard before the birds are spotted. Call note is a metallic *pink*.

Adult male (left). Smaller and shorter-tailed than Red-winged Blackbird. Entirely black below. Back of head golden-buff. Extensive white on shoulders, lower back and rump. Female/immature (below). Upperparts light olive-brown streaked black. Blackish lateral crown stripes with pale buffy supercilium and central crown stripe.

Red-winged Blackbird

Agelaius phoenixes

L 8" | **WS** 14"

While many birds have names that make no sense, it's hard to come up with a more perfectly named bird than this species. Red-winged Blackbirds are widespread and abundant all across North America and Oregon is no exception in this regard. This species can be found virtually anywhere that there is water and vegetation. Male Red-wingeds are among the first birds to stake out territories and start singing each spring, be that from a utility wire, a fencepost or the top of a cattail. They are common breeders in every Oregon county and nest abundantly around larger permanent wetlands and marshes. During fall and winter they form large feeding flocks, often gathering around grain elevators, dairy farms and other places where grain is likely to be spilled. The distinctive *conk-a-ree* song can be heard any time of year. They also give a wide variety of other whistled and scolding calls.

Adult male. Medium-sized all-black bird with conspicuous red wing patch that is bordered with yellow at the bottom. All-dark bill tapers to a sharp point.

Adult female. Noticeably smaller than the male. Heavily streaked with dark chocolate brown and buff. Subtle whitish wing bars. Face sometimes has a peachy or rusty wash. Bold whitish to buffy supercilium. Often mistaken for some type of sparrow.

Tricolored Blackbird

Agelaius tricolor

L 8" | **WS** 14"

Although closely related and virtually identical to the Red-winged Blackbird, the Tricolored Blackbird's range is limited to the Pacific Coast. Tricoloreds have a spotty distribution away from central California, with disjunct breeding clusters scattered north and south through the mid-section of Oregon. Klamath County is a traditional stronghold with several active colonies most years. They are also known to nest in Wasco, Sherman, Umatilla, Crook and Wheeler Counties. Tricolored Blackbirds are more gregarious and colonial than other blackbirds, forming incredibly dense colonies of many dozens of birds in tiny marshes that might support only one or two pairs of more territorial Red-winged Blackbirds. In flight, Tricoloreds form much tighter oval, or ball-shaped flocks than other blackbirds. Their assorted vocalizations include one that is truly unique. They make an odd nasal complaining sound, similar to what might be heard from a kitten being squeezed too tightly.

Adult male. Male Tricolored is similar to male Red-winged Blackbird, but shoulder patch is crimson rather than orangish-red and the border is gleaming white rather than yellow or cream-colored. Overall slightly glossier than Red-winged.

Adult female. While similar in pattern to female Red-winged, Tricolored female is 'colder' ashy-gray, with no brown or buff tones in its plumage. Under parts less streaked and solidly dark on the lower breast and belly. Wing bars whitish to pale gray.

Western Meadowlark

Sturnella negletta

L 8.25" | **WS** 16"

Like many of the Oregon's grassland birds, Western Meadowlarks are thriving east of the Cascades, while westside breeding
numbers are steadily declining as grassland habitats get
converted to various kinds of development and agricultural use.
Meadowlarks are migratory, with most eastside nesters leaving
the state during winter. Modest numbers remain to winter on
the westside. Nests are built on the ground and are well-hidden
under thick clumps of grass. Oregon's state bird was once found
in abundance in the Willamette Valley, but is now generally
scarce there, particularly from Salem northward. Its loud song
starts with clear whistled introductory notes that are followed
by a slightly descending gurgling warble. It can be heard from
upwards of a quarter mile away. In the eastside grasslands and
sagebrush steppe where meadowlarks are most abundant it is
pretty typical to hear 3-4 singing males (sometimes more) any
place that one stops to listen. Common call notes are throaty
chuck and plaintive whistled *peeur*.

Adult. Plump, short-tailed
robin-sized bird. Under parts
mostly bright yellow with distinctive
black "V" across breast. Flanks
creamy with heavy brown streaking.
Head has brown and whitish
stripes. Long thin sharply pointed
bill. Earthy-brown upper parts
heavily patterned.

Yellow-headed Blackbird
Xanthocephalus xanthocephalus

L 8-10" | **WS** 17"

Like the Red-winged Blackbird, this bird has an intuitive and
simple name. Yellow-headed Blackbirds have long been abundant breeders in the large basin marsh complexes throughout
eastern Oregon, but until fairly recently were scarce nesters
west of the Cascades. With the enhancement of many existing
marshes and the development of several new wetlands in the
Willamette Valley, this species now nests regularly at several
sites in western Oregon. Yellow-headed Blackbirds leave the
state to winter. They seem to prefer expansive cattail marshes
and are not often found at sites that lack cattails. The song of
the Yellow-headed Blackbird is distinctive. It starts with a few
somewhat musical introductory notes then quickly devolves
into a series of raspy screeching notes that could use some
lubrication. Typical call is dry stuttered, or double-noted
che-check.

Adult male. Large jay-sized blackbird with
bright golden-yellow head, neck and bib
that extends well down onto the breast. In
flight, note white wing patches. Thick-
based black bill tapers to sharp point.

Adult female. Noticeably smaller than male.
Overall plumage is dark chocolate-brown.
Duller yellow is restricted to the face, throat
and upper breast. Thick-based black bill
tapers to sharp point.

Brewer's Blackbird

Euphagus cyanocephalus

L 8-10" | **WS** 15"

This species is an adaptable habitat generalist as likely to be found in a montane meadow as it is in a suburban grocery store parking lot. Brewer's Blackbirds occupy much drier habitats than other Oregon blackbirds. They are common breeders statewide, particular around human habitation. Brewer's nest in dense conifer shrubs and trees and are less likely to be seen in marshy habitats. They commonly feed along the shoulders of highways and on manicured lawns in parks and on golf courses. Disturbed open areas from sea level to timberline are attractive to Brewer's Blackbirds. Song is rising metallic *cha-reeee* than can be somewhat raspy or higher-pitched and clearer. Calls include slightly grating *chit* and a softer *chuck*.

Adult male. Highly iridescent blackbird, with greenish gloss on back, wings, and underparts with the head showing a more bluish-purple gloss. Eye is creamy or near white.

Adult female. Almost entirely medium earthy-brown, slightly paler on breast and bellow. Dark eye. All-dark bill.

Brown-headed Cowbird

Molothrus ater

L 8" | **WS** 11-14"

Nomadic birds that are best known for laying their eggs in the nests of other birds, Brown-headed Cowbirds are abundant and widespread in Oregon April–September. During the nesting season they are found throughout the state from sea level to near timberline. About the only habitat they don't use is closed forest where there are no cleared or open areas. Since cowbirds don't build nests of their own, they are not tied to a particular breeding habitat. They deposit eggs in the nests of smaller birds, which results in the larger cowbird chick dominating other nestlings and getting most of the food. Yellow Warblers and Warbling Vireos are frequent targets of Brown-headed Cowbird nest parasitism. Most cowbirds leave Oregon during the winter, but they can be found in mixed flocks with other blackbirds around dairy barns and stockyards. Song is rising series of 4–5 thin high-pitched whistled notes. Calls include a thin whistled sweeee and a fast sputter usually done in flight.

Adult female. Entirely medium dirt-brown, with dark eye and stubby conical bill.

Adult male. Small blackbird with a dark chocolate-brown head and stubby conical bill.

Juvenile. Aa very scaly looking version of the female. This plumage often stumps birders who are unfamiliar with it.

Bullock's Oriole

Icterus bullockii

L 7″ | **WS** 12″

This is Oregon's only expected oriole and the one bright orange bird found regularly in the state. Spring migrant Bullock's Orioles arrive by late April and quickly start setting up territories. Their well-constructed sock-shaped nests often remain intact long after they were used. West of the Cascades, Bullock's Orioles breed most commonly in cottonwood gallery forests and other riparian corridors lined with cottonwoods and willows. They also nest in stands of mature Oregon white oak. On the more arid eastside pairs of Bullock's occupy the yards of nearly every farmstead and ranch. They also nest commonly in smaller towns east of the Cascades. Song is a blend chattered notes, squeaky whistled notes and a burry trill. Most common vocalization is harsh chatter.

Adult male. Glowing orange below. Throat, crown, nape, back, and wings black. Black line through eye. Large white patch on median and greater wing coverts.

Adult female. Mostly dingy grayish on upper parts, lower breast, and belly. Head and upper breast dull orangish-yellow. Tail is olive-yellow.

Orange-crowned Warbler
Oreothlypis celata

L 5" | **WS** 7.25"

Far less colorful than most members of the warbler family,
this species is virtually devoid of field marks; even the orange
crown is rarely visible. Orange-crowned Warblers are abundant
spring migrants from late March well into May, particular west
of the Cascades. They nest commonly in regenerating forest
openings and streamside willows and alders in low-to-mid
elevation mountains and foothills. They are rare but regular
in westside lowlands in winter. This species feeds deliberately,
creeping along a branch to glean insects and larvae from the
underside of leaves. Song is a fast, junco-like trill that drops in
pitch near the end.

Adult. Extremely pointed, thin black bill. Yellow-green overall and brighter yellow below
west of the Cascades, duller olive-green with more gray on the head in northeastern
Oregon mountains.

Nashville Warbler

Oreothlypis ruficapilla

L 4.75" | **WS** 7.5"

Primarily upslope breeders in Oregon, Nashville Warblers
nest in drier woodlands, especially forests featuring a mix of
conifers, oak, or madrone with brushy understory. They are
uncommon to common breeders in the Siskiyou Mountains and
the southern Coast Range and on drier mid-elevation slopes
between 2,000 and 4,000 feet in the Cascades and mountains
farther east. They also breed at lower elevations in the foothills
of the Rogue and Umpqua Valleys, but are not typically found
in the Coast Range north of Eugene. Nashvilles are uncommon
lowland migrants during spring, except along the outer coast,
where they are rare at any season. They are infrequently seen in
fall. The tail is often flipped side to side. Song is a fast *see-bit,
see-bit, see-bit* followed by a lower-pitched trill that slows
slightly at the end.

Adult male. Small, compact warbler.
Well-defined gray hood frames bright yellow
throat. Underparts bright yellow, upperparts
olive-green. Crisp, complete white eye ring.
No wing bars. Female and immature paler,
with more white below.

MacGillivray's Warbler

Geothlypis tolmiei

L 4-6" | **WS** 7.5"

Only when you have learned the song of the MacGillivray's Warbler will you fully appreciate the true abundance of this skulker. Other than the occasional teed-up singing male, MacGillivray's Warblers remain buried in the brush, usually within six feet of the ground. They prefer young second growth and brush along mountain streams, but can be found in almost any forest opening with a dense understory. Regenerating clearcuts and powerline rights of way are good places to look for them. Song starts with three clear *cheer* notes followed by a short, decelerating throaty trill. Pattern suggests a car that won't start. Emphatic, fairly loud chip note.

Adult male. Large, chunky, heavy-billed warbler with slate-gray hood and bib. Blackish lores, conspicuous white eye arcs. Underparts bright yellow. No wing bars. Legs and feet pink.

Adult female/immature. Female and immature have lighter gray heads, with pale ash-gray throat and upper breast. Underparts slightly duller than male's.

Common Yellowthroat

Geothlypis trichas

L 5" | **WS** 6.5"

The loud *witchity, witchity, witchity* of the black-masked Common Yellowthroat is one of first warbler songs heard each spring. Arriving in early April, males almost immediately establish a territory and start singing. Like sparrows or wrens, yellowthroats keep close to the ground and are not often seen in trees. They are found in deep grass and brushy tangles around water, from sea level wetlands to wet montane meadows. Yellowthroats are widespread and abundant in western Oregon, but their distribution is patchy east of the Cascades, where they can be absent from habitat that seems perfect for them. Fall numbers can be impressive, with immatures lingering well into October. Call notes sound like the pluck of a loose guitar string.

Adult male. Male is unmistakable, with distinctive black mask bordered above by white. Bright yellow throat and upper breast. Upperparts olive-green. Pinkish legs and feet.

Adult female. Female nondescript brownish olive-green above. Dull olive-yellowish below, brighter yellow on throat. Plain face. No wing bars. Pink legs and feet. Immature female tawny beneath, with pale throat and complete eye ring.

Yellow Warbler

Setophaga petechia

L 5" | **WS** 8"

Oregon's most widespread breeding warbler nests commonly anywhere there are willows or cottonwoods, from sea level to near timberline. Yellow Warbler territories are small and often tightly packed, resulting in frequent turf wars that involve males chasing one another around. Nowhere is this more readily seen than along the Central Patrol Road through Malheur National Wildlife Refuge. Yellow Warblers are also very abundant along the willow-lined banks of the Blitzen River. Their high-pitched song is highly variable, the most common *sweet, sweet, sweeter than sweet*. Chip note is loud and snappy.

Adult male. Large, entirely yellow warbler with heavy bill. Reddish brown streaking on breast. Plain face accentuates large dark eye. Diffuse yellow eye ring.

Adult female/ immature. Female and immature are paler and more lemon yellow than male. No streaking below. Immatures may be dull olive; usually show white eye ring and diagnostic white edges on tertials.

Yellow-rumped Warbler

Setophaga coronata

L 5.5" | **WS** 9"

Yellow-rumped Warblers are common April and May migrants statewide; breeding is common in conifer forests, especially lodgepole pine and fir and spruce, in most of Oregon's mountains. Fall migrants start appearing about mid-September, and by October numbers can be staggering. They winter commonly in the western Oregon lowlands, particularly in coastal wax myrtle and shore pine habitats. Song is a soft, slightly rising warbled trill. Call note for both populations (subspecies) is a crisp *chek* with Myrtle's being a bit lower-pitched and flatter.

Adult male Audubon's. Male bluish-gray above, with black streaks on back. Bright yellow crown, rump, and breast sides; throat yellow in birds breeding in Oregon. Breast and upper flanks black. White belly and undertail with black streaks.

Adult male Myrtle. Northern breeders average grayer above; throat white. More restricted white in wing.

Winter/immature Audubon's. Winter adult and immature olive-brown to gray-brown above. Pale underparts with variable blurry streaks. Two wing bars.

Black-throated Gray Warbler

Setophaga nigrescens

L 4.5–5" | **WS** 7.5"

The only black and white warbler expected in the state, migrant Black-throated Gray Warblers arrive in western Oregon during the first ten days of April and two or three weeks later east of the Cascades. Small flocks routinely occur at migrant sites such as Skinner Butte in Eugene and Mt. Tabor Park in Portland. Common nesters in the Cascades, Coast Range, and Siskiyou Mountains and their associated foothills, they breed in mid- to low-elevation forests with Douglas-fir, western red cedar, red alder, bigleaf maple, or in drier areas madrone. They are locally uncommon nesters in foothills east of the Cascades, and even breed in juniper-filled canyons in southeastern Oregon. Fall migrants can be found well into October. They rarely winter in Oregon. Song strident, with buzzy trilled notes at the end; often a fast, high-pitched *zicka, zicka, zee, zee, zee.* Call is a soft *thek.*

Adult male. Male with stunning black and white head pattern, black throat. Yellow spot in front of eye. Medium-gray back essentially unstreaked. Underparts white, with heavy black streaks on flanks. Two bold white wing bars.

Adult female/immature. Female and immature with mostly white throat; black in head pattern of male replaced by dark slate-gray. Reduced dark flank streaking. All ages with yellow spot in front of eye.

Townsend's Warbler

Setophaga townsendi

L 4.75″ | **WS** 8″

Among the more stunning and colorful of Oregon's warblers, the Townsend's Warbler is an uncommon to common fir forest breeder along the east slope of the Cascades and in the Ochoco, Blue, and Wallowa Mountains; most of its breeding range lies north of the state. It can be found statewide in spring migration, and is uncommon during winter along the coast and in the valley lowlands of inland western Oregon, often flocking with chickadees and kinglets. Winter feeding flocks occasionally include more than twenty individuals. Interbreeds extensively with the Hermit Warbler, and apparent hybrids are frequently encountered. Song is a slurred string of buzzy notes, ending with *zoo zee*. In migration, the song is less strident and even more slurred. Call a high metallic *zeet*.

Adult male. Male with striking yellow, green, and black pattern. Crown, cheek, and throat black. Face and breast bright yellow. Heavy black flank streaks. Dark olive-green above with faint black streaking. Bold white wing bars.

Adult female/immature. Crown and cheek patch dark olive-green. Throat yellow. Weak necklace of streaks across upper breast on adult, absent on immature. Reduced flank streaking. White outer tail feathers flash in flight.

Hermit Warbler
Setophaga occidentalis

L 5.5" | **WS** 8"

Hermit Warblers breed in mind-numbing numbers in the Cascades, Coast Range, and Siskiyou Mountains, but are tough to see, spending much of their time in the canopy. They inhabit mixed conifer forests generally above 1,500 feet in elevation; their abundance diminishes towards timberline. Densities are greatest where grand fir is prevalent. They arrive in late April, leave by September, and rarely winter in Oregon. Along the crest of the Cascades, Hermits routinely interbreed with Townsend's Warblers, resulting in individuals with intermediate characteristics. "Hermit" Warblers with yellow breasts or noticeable flank streaking are probably hybrids. Variable songs are similar to those of Townsend's and Black-throated Gray Warblers. Buzzy *zeedle, zeedle, zeedle zee-zoo*, with emphasis on the last two notes, is more strident than the Townsend's song and not as fast, buzzy, or high-pitched as Black-throated Gray. Call is a high-pitched, silvery *tseet*.

Adult male. Breeding male has stunning bright yellow head, no cheek patch, and a black throat. Upperparts mostly dark gray with black streaks. Underparts whitish and essentially unmarked. Bold white wing bars. First-year male is slightly duller overall.

Adult female/immature. Female and immature have duller yellow head with no black on throat. Upperparts olive-gray to greenish. May show slightly dusky ear coverts. White outer tail feathers flash in flight.

Wilson's Warbler

Cardellina pusilla

L 4.5" | **WS** 7"

Readily identifiable by its bright yellow plumage and black cap, the Wilson's Warbler breeds abundantly all across Oregon, from boggy wooded bottomlands near sea level to moist-sloped drainages in mountains. Wilson's Warblers are particularly abundant in the northern Coast Range. The first arrivals usually reach western Oregon by the second week of April, and northbound migrants can still be seen passing through Harney County migrant spots in early June. The loud song is a series of *chee, chee, chee, chee* notes, accelerating and slightly dropping in pitch towards the end. Call is a single squeaky *chimp*, very similar to the double-noted call of the Pacific Wren.

Adult male. Bright yellow, with black cap (reduced or absent in female and immature). Tail, longer than in most warblers, frequently flipped side to side.

Western Tanager
Piranga ludoviciana

L 6.5-7.75" | **WS** 11.5"

With its gleaming red head and bright yellow body, the male
Western Tanager seems downlike tropical. This species breeds
commonly in conifers and mixed forests all across Oregon.
Spring migration is protracted, with the earliest birds arriving
on the westside in late April and others still moving through
southeastern Oregon well into June. When cold fronts stall
migrants at their mid-May peak, these colorful birds seem to
hang like Christmas tree ornaments from every tree. Once on
their nesting grounds, Western Tanagers are more often heard
than seen, as they stay high in the canopy. Song has a robin-like
cadence, but the notes are more abrupt, burry and less musical.
There are usually three phrases, *pitik, pituk, pitik,* with
the middle phrase lower in pitch. In flight, often gives a soft,
plaintive *wee*.

Adult male. Male bright
yellow with red head
and black wings.
Immature males similar,
with limited red on head.

Adult female. Thrush-sized
female varies from rich
greenish yellow to dull grayish
and olive. Sturdy bill orangish
beneath; two crisp whitish
wing bars.

Black-headed Grosbeak

Pheucticus melanocephalus

L 7–7.5" | **WS** 12.5"

Singing Black-headed Grosbeaks sound like American Robins that have had too many cups of coffee. It can be a struggle to actually see the well-hidden singer, typically buried in heavy foliage. Migrants arrive in Oregon en masse about the third week of April. Black-headed Grosbeaks breed commonly in a variety of mixed deciduous and coniferous forests and along riparian corridors from nearly 5,000 feet down to sea level. Fall migration stretches well into September. Robin-like song is longer and sung with great vigor at a quick pace. Call is a sharp, squeaky *speek*.

Adult male. Male has black head. Burnt orange breast and flanks transition to yellow on lower belly and undertail. Wings black with broad white wing bars. Heavy conical bill bluish-gray.

Adult female. Strongly patterned head with a conspicuous whitish supercilium. Dull orange breast fades to paler buffy or yellow-orange belly with some fine streaking. Dark streaky upper parts. Wing bars not as broad as on male. Heavy conical bill dark above and paler pinkish below.

Lazuli Bunting

Passerina amoena

L 5-6" | **WS** 8.75"

Perhaps Oregon's most visually stunning bird, a male Lazuli
Bunting in bright sunlight will stop any birder in their tracks.
This sparrow-sized bunting has greatly increased in abundance
in recent years, particularly in the Willamette Valley, where
it was formerly only an uncommon breeder. Lazuli Buntings
now nest commonly statewide except on the outer coast. They
are most abundant along riparian corridors, in regenerating
clearcuts at foothill elevations, and at sites with a mix of
semi-open woodlands and pastures with brushy trees. Song
is a jumbled warble of seven or eight high-pitched squeaky
notes with slight pitch changes. Calls include a sharp *spit* and a
buzzy *zzzt* given in flight.

Adult male. Brilliant azure-blue head and upperparts, broad white wing bars. Upper breast rich buffy-orange. Belly and undertail white. Modest-sized conical bill.

Adult female. Mostly dull tan, with conspicuous pale-buff wing bars. Dull azure-blue shoulder patch and bluish tail.

Acknowledgments

I've often been asked how I came to know what I know about birds and in particular the birds of Oregon. The answer is simple—I have learned virtually all of it from others. Mentoring and passing forward knowledge organically is something birders do. There is always joy in seeing a new bird and at least as much joy in helping another birder see and identify a bird for the first time. Authoring this book has provided an opportunity to honor that tradition.

I am grateful to each and every person who has taught me something about birds over my lifetime. This starts with my parents Harry Irons and Judie Hansen who were my first and most influential mentors. They started me birding about the time I started school. It's hard to imagine what my life might look like without birding and all that they have taught me. Our family first visited Oregon in 1968 when we made a three-week camping/birding tour of the western United States. A year and a half later we would move to Portland. It has been a love affair with the state's birds and Oregon's landscapes ever since.

In 1977 I met David Fix on a Audubon Society of Portland field trip and everything changed. I had a birding peer. He mentored me early on and introduced me to ear-birding and other birders close to our age. Over the next decade, weekends and sometimes weeks were spent on the road birding every corner of Oregon, usually in someone else's car. I would travel hundreds of thousands of miles with Fix, Jeff Gilligan, Mark Koninendyke, Harry Nehls, Owen Schmidt, Steve Heinl, Matt Hunter, and others too numerous to mention. I came to know many new places and the birds that inhabited them, gathering nuggets of knowledge from others every step of the way.

Eventually I carved out some space in my life to become a semi-responsible adult and along with that came the most important job of my life–raising my three children, Lucy, Lilly and Stuart. They endured my birding fanaticism as well as kids endure any of their parents' annoying habits. They all love being outside and going camping and as adults they formed their own unique relationships with Oregon's mountains, high desert, and coastline. If I have done one thing right, this would be it. We lost Lilly in 2014, but have since placed a memorial bench at Malheur N.W.R. headquarters and scattered some of her ashes at various sites around Oregon. She is always with us wherever we wander.

For the last nine years I have had one constant birding companion and companion in life. Shawneen Finnegan and I found each other and were instantly smitten in 2009. Since that time we've birded all over the United States laughing, seeing new birds and making new friends everywhere we've traveled. Her connections in the birding world have opened doors and created opportunities (like writing this book) that probably wouldn't have come my way otherwise. I love her and being her Oregon tour guide as she gets to know all the places that I've spent a lifetime exploring.

Finally, I am grateful to George Scott for inviting me to author this book. Writing about Oregon birds and the places that we go to see them reminds me how fortunate I am and have been to live and bird in such a wonderful place.

Dave Irons, June 2018

Scott & Nix Acknowledgments

Many thanks to Jeffrey A. Gordon and Liz Gordon, Ted Floyd, John Lowry, and everyone at the American Birding Association for their good work. Special thanks to Independent Book Publishers (IPG). Thanks to the Cornell Lab of Ornithology for their data sets. We give special thanks to Brian E. Small for his extraordinary photographs and to all the others whose images illuminate this guide. We thank Rick Wright for his work on the manuscript; Paul Pianin and Soren Martin Gonzales for helping with layout, and proofing the galleys; James Montalbano of Terminal Design for his typefaces; Charles Nix for design; and René Nedelkoff and Nancy Heinomen of Four Colour Print Group for help in shepherding this book through print production.

Image Credits

(T) = Top, (B) = Bottom, (L) = Left, (R) = Right; pages with multiple images from one source are indicated by a single credit.

XIII–XXXIII Brian E. Small. **2** Brian E. Small (T), Bob Steele (B). **3–10** Brian E. Small. **11** Brian E. Small (T), Dave Irons (B). **12** Brian E. Small. **13** Brian E. Small (T), Dave Irons (B). **14–26** Brian E. Small. **27** Brian E. Small (T), Joe Fuhrman (B). **28–37** Brian E. Small. **38** Alan Murphy. **39–40** Brian E. Small. **41** Brian E. Small (T), Bob Steele (B). **42–43** Brian E. Small. **44** Brian E. Small (T), Joe Fuhrman (B). **45–54** Brian E. Small. **55** Bob Steele (T), Brian E. Small (B). **56–57** Brian E. Small. **58** Brian E. Small (T), Bob Steele (B). **59–71** Brian E. Small. **72** Brian E. Small (T), Bob Steele (B). **73–82** Brian E. Small. **83** Brian E. Small (T) Dave Irons (B). **84–94** Brian E. Small. **95** Brian E. Small (T), Bob Steele (B). **96** Brian E. Small (T), Bob Steele (B). **97–100** Brian E. Small. **101** Brian E. Small (T), Alvaro Jaramillo (B). **102–105** Brian E. Small. **106** Bob Steele. **107** Alan Murphy (T), Bob Steele (B). **108** Mike Danzenbaker (T), Brian E. Small (B). **109–110** Brian E. Small. **110** Bob Steele (T), Brian E. Small (B). **111–117** Brian E. Small. **118** Brian Patteson/VIREO. **119** Alan Murphy. **120** M. Hale/VIREO. **121** Y. Artukhin/VIREO. **122–139** Brian E. Small. **140** Jim Zipp. **140–141** Brian E. Small. **142** Brian E. Small (L), Jim Zipp (R). **143** Brian E. Small (L), Bob Steele (R). **144** Brian E. Small. **145–146** Bob Steele. **147** Jerry Liguori (L), Brian E. Small (R). **148–175** Brian E. Small. **176** Alan Murphy (L), Brian E. Small (R). **177** Brian E. Small. **178** Brian E. Small, Bob Steele (R). **179–192** Brian E. Small. **193** Bob Steele. **194–203** Brian E. Small. **204** Bob Steele (L), Brian E. Small (R). **205–206** Brian E. Small. **207** Brian E. Small (T), Bob Steele (B). **208–209** Brian E. Small. **210** Bob Steele (L), Brian E. Small (R). **211** Brian E. Small. **212** G. Bartley/VIREO (L), Brian E. Small (R). **213** Alan Murphy (L), Brian E. Small (R). **214** Brian E. Small (T), Alan Murphy (B). **215–216** Brian E. Small. **217** Bob Steele. **218–247** Brian E. Small. **248** Brian E. Small (L), Bob Steele (R). **249–279** Brian E. Small. **280** Dave Irons. **281–306** Brian E. Small.

Official Checklist of Oregon Birds

OREGON BIRD RECORDS COMMITTEE

*   A review species. At least one record has been verified by photograph, specimen, or video/audio recording: 138 species.

**   A review species. Sight records only, no video/audio verification: 15 species.

E   Extirpated. No modern records: California Condor and Sharp-tailed Grouse; Northern Bobwhite –no established population.

I   Introduced: 8 species.

This list is updated through the AOU 58th Supplement, July 2017.

536 total species.

Order ANSERIFORMES
FAMILY ANATIDAE
Subfamily Dendrocygninae
☐ * Black-bellied Whistling-Duck
☐ * Fulvous Whistling-Duck

Subfamily Anserinae
☐ Emperor Goose
☐ Snow Goose
☐ Ross's Goose
☐ Greater White-fronted Goose
☐ * Tundra Bean-Goose
☐ Brant
☐ Cackling Goose
☐ Canada Goose
☐ Trumpeter Swan
☐ Tundra Swan
☐ * Whooper Swan

Subfamily Anatinae
☐ Wood Duck
☐ * Baikal Teal
☐ * Garganey
☐ Blue-winged Teal
☐ Cinnamon Teal
☐ Northern Shoveler
☐ Gadwall
☐ * Falcated Duck
☐ Eurasian Wigeon
☐ American Wigeon
☐ Mallard

☐ * American Black Duck
☐ Northern Pintail
☐ Green-winged Teal
☐ Canvasback
☐ Redhead
☐ Ring-necked Duck
☐ Tufted Duck
☐ Greater Scaup
☐ Lesser Scaup
☐ * Steller's Eider
☐ * King Eider
☐ * Common Eider
☐ Harlequin Duck
☐ Surf Scoter
☐ White-winged Scoter
☐ * Common Scoter
☐ Black Scoter
☐ Long-tailed Duck
☐ Bufflehead
☐ Common Goldeneye
☐ Barrow's Goldeneye
☐ * Smew
☐ Hooded Merganser
☐ Common Merganser
☐ Red-breasted Merganser
☐ Ruddy Duck

Order GALLIFORMES
FAMILY ODONTOPHORIDAE
☐ Mountain Quail

☐ IE Northern Bobwhite
☐ California Quail

FAMILY PHASIANIDAE
Subfamily Phasianinae

☐ I Chukar
☐ I Gray Partridge
☐ I Ring-necked Pheasant

Subfamily Tetraoninae

☐ Ruffed Grouse
☐ Greater Sage-Grouse
☐ Spruce Grouse
☐ Dusky Grouse
☐ Sooty Grouse
☐ *E Sharp-tailed Grouse

Subfamily Meleagridinae

☐ I Wild Turkey

Order PODICIPEDIFORMES
FAMILY PODICIPEDIDAE

☐ Pied-billed Grebe
☐ Horned Grebe
☐ Red-necked Grebe Eared Grebe
☐ Western Grebe
☐ Clark's Grebe

Order COLUMBIFORMES
FAMILY COLUMBIDAE

☐ I Rock Pigeon
☐ Band-tailed Pigeon
☐ I Eurasian Collared-Dove
☐ * Common Ground-Dove
☐ White-winged Dove
☐ Mourning Dove

Order CUCULIFORMES
FAMILY CUCULIDAE
Subfamily Cuculinae

☐ * Yellow-billed Cuckoo

Subfamily Neomorphinae

☐ ** Greater Roadrunner

Order CAPRIMULGIFORMES
FAMILY CAPRIMULGIDAE
Subfamily Chordeilinae

☐ * Lesser Nighthawk
☐ Common Nighthawk

Subfamily Caprimulginae

☐ Common Poorwill
☐ * Eastern Whip-poor-will

Order APODIFORMES
FAMILY APODIDAE
Subfamily Cypseloidinae

☐ Black Swift

Subfamily Chaeturinae

☐ * Chimney Swift
☐ Vaux's Swift

Subfamily Apodinae

☐ White-throated Swift

FAMILY TROCHILIDAE
Subfamily Trochilinae

☐ * Ruby-throated Hummingbird
☐ Black-chinned Hummingbird
☐ Anna's Hummingbird
☐ Costa's Hummingbird
☐ Broad-tailed Hummingbird
☐ Rufous Hummingbird
☐ Allen's Hummingbird
☐ Calliope Hummingbird
☐ * Broad-billed Hummingbird

Order GRUIFORMES
FAMILY RALLIDAE

☐ Yellow Rail
☐ Virginia Rail
☐ Sora
☐ *Common Gallinule
☐ American Coot

FAMILY GRUIDAE
Subfamily Gruinae

☐ Sandhill Crane

Order CHARADRIIFORMES
FAMILY RECURVIROSTRIDAE

☐ Black-necked Stilt
☐ American Avocet

FAMILY HAEMATOPODIDAE

☐ Black Oystercatcher

FAMILY CHARADRIIDAE
Subfamily Charadriinae

☐ Black-bellied Plover
☐ American Golden-Plover
☐ Pacific Golden-Plover
☐ * Lesser Sand-Plover
☐ Snowy Plover
☐ * Wilson's Plover
☐ Semipalmated Plover
☐ ** Piping Plover

- [ ] Killdeer
- [ ] * Mountain Plover
- [ ] * Eurasian Dotterel

FAMILY SCOLOPACIDAE
Subfamily Numeniinae

- [ ] Upland Sandpiper
- [ ] * Bristle-thighed Curlew
- [ ] Whimbrel
- [ ] Long-billed Curlew

Subfamily Limosinae

- [ ] * Bar-tailed Godwit
- [ ] * Hudsonian Godwit
- [ ] Marbled Godwit

Subfamily Arenariinae

- [ ] Ruddy Turnstone
- [ ] Black Turnstone
- [ ] * Great Knot
- [ ] Red Knot
- [ ] Surfbird
- [ ] Ruff
- [ ] Sharp-tailed Sandpiper
- [ ] Stilt Sandpiper
- [ ] * Curlew Sandpiper
- [ ] *Long-toed Stint
- [ ] *Red-necked Stint
- [ ] Sanderling
- [ ] Dunlin
- [ ] Rock Sandpiper
- [ ] Baird's Sandpiper
- [ ] * Little Stint
- [ ] Least Sandpiper
- [ ] * White-rumped Sandpiper
- [ ] Buff-breasted Sandpiper
- [ ] Pectoral Sandpiper
- [ ] Semipalmated Sandpiper
- [ ] Western Sandpiper

Subfamily Scolopacinae

- [ ] Short-billed Dowitcher
- [ ] Long-billed Dowitcher
- [ ] * Jack Snipe
- [ ] Wilson's Snipe

Subfamily Tringinae

- [ ] Spotted Sandpiper
- [ ] Solitary Sandpiper
- [ ] Wandering Tattler
- [ ] Lesser Yellowlegs
- [ ] Willet
- [ ] * Spotted Redshank

- [ ] Greater Yellowlegs
- [ ] * Wood Sandpiper
- [ ] Wilson's Phalarope
- [ ] Red-necked Phalarope
- [ ] Red Phalarope

FAMILY STERCORARIIDAE

- [ ] South Polar Skua
- [ ] Pomarine Jaeger
- [ ] Parasitic Jaeger
- [ ] Long-tailed Jaeger

FAMILY ALCIDAE

- [ ] Common Murre
- [ ] *Thick-billed Murre
- [ ] Pigeon Guillemot
- [ ] * Long-billed Murrelet
- [ ] Marbled Murrelet
- [ ] Scripps's Murrelet
- [ ] * Guadalupe Murrelet
- [ ] Ancient Murrelet
- [ ] Cassin's Auklet
- [ ] Parakeet Auklet
- [ ] Rhinoceros Auklet
- [ ] Horned Puffin
- [ ] Tufted Puffin

FAMILY LARIDAE
Subfamily Larinae

- [ ] Black-legged Kittiwake
- [ ] * Red-legged Kittiwake
- [ ] Sabine's Gull
- [ ] Bonaparte's Gull
- [ ] * Black-headed Gull
- [ ] * Little Gull
- [ ] * Ross's Gull
- [ ] * Laughing Gull
- [ ] Franklin's Gull
- [ ] Heermann's Gull
- [ ] Mew Gull
- [ ] Ring-billed Gull
- [ ] Western Gull
- [ ] California Gull
- [ ] Herring Gull
- [ ] Iceland Gull
- [ ] * Lesser Black-backed Gull
- [ ] * Slaty-backed Gull
- [ ] Glaucous-winged Gull
- [ ] Glaucous Gull

Subfamily Sterninae

- [ ] * Least Tern

☐ Caspian Tern
☐ Black Tern
☐ Common Tern
☐ Arctic Tern
☐ Forster's Tern
☐ Elegant Tern

Subfamily Rynchopinae

☐ ** Black Skimmer

Order PHAETHONTIFORMES
FAMILY PHAETHONTIDAE

☐ * Red-billed Tropicbird

Order GAVIIFORMES
FAMILY GAVIIDAE

☐ Red-throated Loon
☐ * Arctic Loon
☐ Pacific Loon
☐ Common Loon
☐ Yellow-billed Loon

Order PROCELLARIIFORMES
AMILY DIOMEDEIDAE

☐ * White-capped Albatross
☐ * Wandering Albatross
☐ Laysan Albatross
☐ Black-footed Albatross
☐ * Short-tailed Albatross

FAMILY PROCELLARIIDAE

☐ Northern Fulmar
☐ Murphy's Petrel
☐ Mottled Petrel
☐ ** Juan Fernandez Petrel
☐ *Hawaiian Petrel
☐ * Cook's Petrel
☐ ** Stejneger's Petrel
☐ ** Streaked Shearwater
☐ * Wedge-tailed Shearwater
☐ Buller's Shearwater
☐ Short-tailed Shearwater
☐ Sooty Shearwater
☐ * Great Shearwater
☐ Pink-footed Shearwater
☐ Flesh-footed Shearwater
☐ Manx Shearwater
☐ ** Black-vented Shearwater

FAMILY HYDROBATIDAE

☐ * Wilson's Storm-Petrel
☐ Fork-tailed Storm-Petrel
☐ ** Ringed Storm-Petrel

☐ Leach's Storm-Petrel
☐ * Ashy Storm-Petrel
☐ * Black Storm-Petrel

Order SULIFORMES
FAMILY FREGATIDAE

☐ * Magnificent Frigatebird

FAMILY SULIDAE

☐ * Masked Booby
☐ * Blue-footed Booby
☐ * Brown Booby

FAMILY PHALACROCORACIDAE

☐ Brandt's Cormorant
☐ Double-crested Cormorant
☐ Pelagic Cormorant

Order PELECANIFORMES
FAMILY PELECANIDAE

☐ American White Pelican
☐ Brown Pelican

FAMILY ARDEIDAE

☐ American Bittern
☐ Least Bittern
☐ Great Blue Heron
☐ Great Egret
☐ Snowy Egret
☐ * Little Blue Heron
☐ * Tricolored Heron
☐ Cattle Egret
☐ Green Heron
☐ Black-crowned Night-Heron
☐ * Yellow-crowned Night-Heron

FAMILY THRESKIORNITHIDAE
Subfamily Threskiornithinae

☐ * White Ibis
☐ * Glossy Ibis
☐ White-faced Ibis

Order CATHARTIFORMES
FAMILY CATHARTIDAE

☐ Turkey Vulture
☐ *E California Condor

Order ACCIPITRIFORMES
FAMILY PANDIONIDAE

☐ Osprey

FAMILY ACCIPITRIDAE

☐ White-tailed Kite
☐ Bald Eagle

☐ Northern Harrier
☐ Sharp-shinned Hawk
☐ Cooper's Hawk
☐ Northern Goshawk
☐ Red-shouldered Hawk
☐ Broad-winged Hawk
☐ Swainson's Hawk
☐ Red-tailed Hawk
☐ Rough-legged Hawk
☐ Ferruginous Hawk
☐ Golden Eagle

Order STRIGIFORMES
FAMILY TYTONIDAE

☐ Barn Owl

FAMILY STRIGIDAE

☐ Flammulated Owl
☐ Western Screech-Owl
☐ Great Horned Owl
☐ Snowy Owl
☐ *Northern Hawk Owl
☐ Northern Pygmy-Owl
☐ Burrowing Owl
☐ Spotted Owl
☐ Barred Owl
☐ Great Gray Owl
☐ Long-eared Owl
☐ Short-eared Owl
☐ Boreal Owl
☐ Northern Saw-whet Owl

Order CORACIIFORMES
FAMILY ALCEDINIDAE
Subfamily Cerylinae

☐ Belted Kingfisher

Order PICIFORMES
FAMILY PICIDAE
Subfamily Picinae

☐ Lewis's Woodpecker
☐ * Red-headed Woodpecker
☐ Acorn Woodpecker
☐ * Red-bellied Woodpecker
☐ Williamson's Sapsucker
☐ Yellow-bellied Sapsucker
☐ Red-naped Sapsucker
☐ Red-breasted Sapsucker
☐ * Nuttall's Woodpecker
☐ Downy Woodpecker
☐ Hairy Woodpecker
☐ White-headed Woodpecker

☐ American Three-toed Woodpecker
☐ Black-backed Woodpecker
☐ Northern Flicker
☐ Pileated Woodpecker

Order FALCONIFORMES
FAMILY FALCONIDAE
Subfamily Falconinae

☐ *Crested Caracara
☐ American Kestrel
☐ Merlin
☐ Gyrfalcon
☐ Peregrine Falcon
☐ Prairie Falcon

Order PASSERIFORMES
FAMILY TYRANNIDAE
Subfamily Fluvicolinae

☐ Olive-sided Flycatcher
☐ Western Wood-Pewee
☐ * Eastern Wood-Pewee
☐ * Alder Flycatcher
☐ Willow Flycatcher
☐ Least Flycatcher
☐ Hammond's Flycatcher
☐ Gray Flycatcher
☐ Dusky Flycatcher
☐ Pacific-slope Flycatcher
☐ Cordilleran Flycatcher
☐ Black Phoebe
☐ * Eastern Phoebe
☐ Say's Phoebe
☐ * Vermilion Flycatcher

Subfamily Tyranninae

☐ * Dusky-capped Flycatcher
☐ Ash-throated Flycatcher
☐ * Great Crested Flycatcher
☐ Tropical Kingbird
☐ * Cassin's Kingbird
☐ Western Kingbird
☐ Eastern Kingbird
☐ * Scissor-tailed Flycatcher
☐ ** Fork-tailed Flycatcher

FAMILY LANIIDAE

☐ Loggerhead Shrike
☐ Northern Shrike

FAMILY VIREONIDAE

☐ * White-eyed Vireo
☐ ** Bell's Vireo

- ☐ Hutton's Vireo
- ☐ * Yellow-throated Vireo
- ☐ Cassin's Vireo
- ☐ * Blue-headed Vireo
- ☐ * Plumbeous Vireo
- ☐ * Philadelphia Vireo
- ☐ Warbling Vireo
- ☐ Red-eyed Vireo

FAMILY CORVIDAE

- ☐ Gray Jay
- ☐ Pinyon Jay
- ☐ Steller's Jay
- ☐ Blue Jay
- ☐ California Scrub-Jay
- ☐ Clark's Nutcracker
- ☐ Black-billed Magpie
- ☐ American Crow
- ☐ Common Raven

FAMILY ALAUDIDAE

- ☐ Horned Lark

FAMILY HIRUNDINIDAE
Subfamily Hirundininae

- ☐ Purple Martin
- ☐ Tree Swallow
- ☐ Violet-green Swallow
- ☐ Northern Rough-winged Swallow
- ☐ Bank Swallow
- ☐ Cliff Swallow
- ☐ Barn Swallow

FAMILY PARIDAE

- ☐ Black-capped Chickadee
- ☐ Mountain Chickadee
- ☐ Chestnut-backed Chickadee
- ☐ Oak Titmouse
- ☐ Juniper Titmouse

FAMILY AEGITHALIDAE

- ☐ Bushtit

FAMILY SITTIDAE
Subfamily Sittinae

- ☐ Red-breasted Nuthatch
- ☐ White-breasted Nuthatch
- ☐ Pygmy Nuthatch

FAMILY CERTHIIDAE
Subfamily Certhiinae

- ☐ Brown Creeper

FAMILY TROGLODYTIDAE

- ☐ Rock Wren
- ☐ Canyon Wren
- ☐ House Wren
- ☐ Pacific Wren
- ☐ * Sedge Wren
- ☐ Marsh Wren
- ☐ Bewick's Wren

FAMILY POLIOPTILIDAE

- ☐ Blue-gray Gnatcatcher

FAMILY CINCLIDAE

- ☐ American Dipper

FAMILY REGULIDAE

- ☐ Golden-crowned Kinglet
- ☐ Ruby-crowned Kinglet

FAMILY SYLVIIDAE

- ☐ Wrentit

FAMILY MUSCICAPIDAE

- ☐ * Red-flanked Bluetail
- ☐ * Northern Wheatear

FAMILY TURDIDAE

- ☐ Western Bluebird
- ☐ Mountain Bluebird
- ☐ Townsend's Solitaire
- ☐ Veery
- ☐ * Gray-cheeked Thrush
- ☐ Swainson's Thrush
- ☐ Hermit Thrush
- ☐ * Wood Thrush
- ☐ American Robin
- ☐ Varied Thrush

FAMILY MIMIDAE

- ☐ Gray Catbird
- ☐ ** Curve-billed Thrasher
- ☐ Brown Thrasher
- ☐ * California Thrasher
- ☐ Sage Thrasher
- ☐ Northern Mockingbird

FAMILY STURNIDAE

- ☐ I European Starling

FAMILY BOMBYCILLIDAE

- ☐ Bohemian Waxwing
- ☐ Cedar Waxwing

FAMILY PTILIOGONATIDAE

☐ * Phainopepla

FAMILY PASSERIDAE

☐ I House Sparrow

FAMILY MOTACILLIDAE

☐ * Eastern Yellow Wagtail
☐ * White Wagtail
☐ * Red-throated Pipit
☐ American Pipit
☐ * Sprague's Pipit

FAMILY FRINGILLIDAE
Subfamily Fringillinae

☐ * Brambling

Subfamily Carduelinae

☐ Evening Grosbeak
☐ Pine Grosbeak
☐ Gray-crowned Rosy-Finch
☐ Black Rosy-Finch
☐ House Finch
☐ Purple Finch
☐ Cassin's Finch
☐ Common Redpoll
☐ ** Hoary Redpoll
☐ Red Crossbill
☐ White-winged Crossbill
☐ Pine Siskin
☐ Lesser Goldfinch
☐ * Lawrence's Goldfinch
☐ American Goldfinch

FAMILY CALCARIIDAE

☐ Lapland Longspur
☐ Chestnut-collared Longspur
☐ * Smith's Longspur
☐ * McCown's Longspur
☐ Snow Bunting
☐ * McKay's Bunting

FAMILY EMBERIZIDAE

☐ * Little Bunting
☐ * Rustic Bunting

FAMILY PASSERELLIDAE

☐ Green-tailed Towhee
☐ Spotted Towhee
☐ * Eastern Towhee
☐ California Towhee

☐ * Cassin's Sparrow
☐ American Tree Sparrow
☐ Chipping Sparrow
☐ Clay-colored Sparrow
☐ Brewer's Sparrow
☐ * Black-chinned Sparrow
☐ Vesper Sparrow
☐ Lark Sparrow
☐ Black-throated Sparrow
☐ Sagebrush Sparrow
☐ Lark Bunting
☐ Savannah Sparrow
☐ Grasshopper Sparrow
☐ * LeConte's Sparrow
☐ Fox Sparrow
☐ Song Sparrow
☐ Lincoln's Sparrow
☐ Swamp Sparrow
☐ White-throated Sparrow
☐ Harris's Sparrow
☐ White-crowned Sparrow
☐ Golden-crowned Sparrow
☐ Dark-eyed Junco

FAMILY ICTERIIDAE

☐ Yellow-breasted Chat

FAMILY ICTERIDAE

☐ Yellow-headed Blackbird
☐ Bobolink
☐ Western Meadowlark
☐ * Orchard Oriole
☐ Hooded Oriole
☐ * Streak-backed Oriole
☐ Bullock's Oriole
☐ *Baltimore Oriole
☐ *Scott's Oriole
☐ Red-winged Blackbird
☐ Tricolored Blackbird
☐ Brown-headed Cowbird
☐ Rusty Blackbird
☐ Brewer's Blackbird
☐ * Common Grackle
☐ Great-tailed Grackle

FAMILY PARULIDAE

☐ Ovenbird
☐ ** Worm-eating Warbler
☐ * Louisiana Waterthrush
☐ Northern Waterthrush

☐ * Golden-winged Warbler
☐ * Blue-winged Warbler
☐ Black-and-white Warbler
☐ * Prothonotary Warbler
☐ Tennessee Warbler
☐ Orange-crowned Warbler
☐ * Lucy's Warbler
☐ Nashville Warbler
☐ * Virginia's Warbler
☐ MacGillivray's Warbler
☐ ** Mourning Warbler
☐ * Kentucky Warbler
☐ Common Yellowthroat
☐ * Hooded Warbler
☐ American Redstart
☐ * Cape May Warbler
☐ Northern Parula
☐ Magnolia Warbler
☐ * Bay-breasted Warbler
☐ *Blackburnian Warbler
☐ Yellow Warbler
☐ Chestnut-sided Warbler
☐ Blackpoll Warbler
☐ Black-throated Blue Warbler
☐ Palm Warbler
☐ * Pine Warbler
☐ Yellow-rumped Warbler
☐ * Yellow-throated Warbler
☐ * Prairie Warbler
☐ Black-throated Gray Warbler
☐ Townsend's Warbler
☐ Hermit Warbler
☐ * Black-throated Green Warbler
☐ * Canada Warbler
☐ Wilson's Warbler
☐ ** Painted Redstart

FAMILY CARDINALIDAE

☐ * Summer Tanager
☐ * Scarlet Tanager
☐ Western Tanager
☐ * Pyrrhuloxia
☐ Rose-breasted Grosbeak
☐ Black-headed Grosbeak
☐ * Blue Grosbeak
☐ Lazuli Bunting
☐ Indigo Bunting
☐ * Painted Bunting
☐ * Dickcissel

Species Index